Shared Wisdom

Tips from Business Experts on How YOU Can Achieve Success

Red Penguin
BOOKS

Library of Congress Control Number: 2022900962

ISBN

Print 978-1-63777-219-5

Digital 978-1-63777-220-1

Contents

Foreword
Ramon Ray, Founder of Smart Hustle

Loneliness is a real thing. In business, especially for very small businesses, loneliness is an epidemic. You're sitting in your home office, alone. You're sitting at the dining room table, all alone. You talk to your family, and they simply don't understand you or what you're going through.

This is why smart business owners look for associations, networking groups, and online discussion forums to join.

We want to surround ourselves with other humans who we can be around. But not just humans, other business owners and working professionals who can help us grow.

They can challenge our assumptions. Make us laugh. Give us feedback. Affirm our guesses.

In 1995, *Fast Company Magazine* had an email discussion group called Company of Friends, spanning across the USA in various geographic segments, and possibly the world. This group birthed friendships and professional relationships amongst creators, freelancers, and corporate employees. An eclectic community of professionals who didn't want to be lonely. Who wanted to grow together.

At some point, *Fast Company* closed down Company of Friends. What would happen to our online discussions? To our in-person meetings?

Adrian Miller, a long-time member of the NYC Company of Friends had a solution. She created her own network, Adrian's Network.

Today, 13 years later, Adrian's Network brings together working professionals and business owners for real-time discussions to help us grow our businesses.

From in-person "brown bag lunches," to online Zoom calls, to beach get-togethers, to Facebook groups, to telephone calls and a powerful email list, over the years Adrian's Network has been THE community of support and camaraderie for so many.

When I was looking for something to show appreciation, I found it in A's Net. Seeking to build my next great website, I found it in A's Net. Wanting to get advice on if it was "unfocused," I found that voice of wisdom on A's Net.

Whether you're trying to grow as an individual or you want to succeed in your career or you want to grow your business, you need input from others.

That input from others could be in a book, podcast, or event.

It's also very important to build long term relationships with people you trust. It's important to have an oasis of humans you can turn to and share and laugh and cry with.

Growing your business alone is tough - maybe impossible.

There's an African proverb (according to Google) which says you can go fast alone, or you can go far together.

Which way do you want to go? Fast or far?

It's a choice.

Adrian Miller made her choice in 2008. Today you can make your choice in how you want to grow your business, who you want to grow it with, and who you want to serve.

Now, some of the professionals that Adrian has aligned herself with over the years are sharing their expertise in this powerful new book, *Shared Wisdom: Tips From Business Experts on How You Can Achieve Success*. Within these pages, you can get a flavor for the brilliance that exists in this group of business experts.

You can find information on a wealth of topics, like networking, public speaking, communicating effectively, writing a book to bring attention to your business, and so much more.

Enjoy this book. Use it. Learn from it. You'll be learning from the best!

Speaking Tips Every
Entrepreneur Needs to Master
Diane DiResta

Love it or hate it, you can no longer avoid public speaking. If you're an entrepreneur, speaking is one of the most powerful and cost-effective marketing strategies. Are you leveraging public speaking to grow your business?

If not, why not? There are two major reasons entrepreneurs avoid speaking.

1. Fear. It's not a secret that public speaking is among people's greatest fears. When I wrote my book, *Knockout Presentations,* I surveyed people about why they were afraid to speak. The answers boiled down to one overarching theme. It was the fear of humiliation. The good news is that nervousness can be managed and humiliation can be avoided if you know recovery strategies.

2. Ignorance. Entrepreneurs may not know how to organize their thoughts or the basic skills of good delivery. I've seen

them struggle to introduce themselves and their services. These skills can be taught. Gifted speakers are born, but effective speakers are made.

Public speaking confidence involves two things: mindset and skill set.

So, let's address the first obstacle-fear. I once told an audience that the meaning of FEAR was False Evidence Appearing Real. Someone yelled out, "That's your definition of FEAR? Mine is "Forget everything and run!" (He actually used an expletive). Here's the truth. When you're very nervous, you're being self-centered. It's all about Me, Myself, and I. You're living in the future, thinking about what could go wrong. "Oh, I hope I don't blank out." "I hope I don't choke up." I say, GET OVER YOURSELF! It's not about you, it's about them--the audience. Put your focus on them. How can you make them feel comfortable? How can you make them smile?

The goal is to move from living in the future to coming back to the present moment. The way to do that is with the breath. Practice simple breathing exercises such as Square Breathing. You can find these exercises on YouTube and in Ch.3 of *Knockout Presentations*. Breathing will slow down your pounding heart and ground your energy.

Another tip for managing nervousness is to prepare and rehearse out loud. When it comes to public speaking, it's 90% preparation and 10% delivery. The more you know your material, the more confident you'll feel.

And finally, what are the messages you're giving yourself? When I coach presenters, we identify their limiting beliefs, and we change them to more powerful affirmations. I remember when I volunteered to do a 10-minute presentation for the National Speakers Association. I started to get very nervous. Afterall, these were professional speakers. They saw world class speakers at annual conferences. I told my friend, "I'm so nervous. Why did I volunteer? I can't wait until tomorrow is over." She grabbed me by the shoulders and said, "Diane, don't do that to yourself. You're not nervous. You're energized!" So, I went home and kept saying "I'm energized. I'm energized." The next day I gave my presentation, and it went well.

What limiting words are you saying about yourself? What can you say that's empowering?

It's not enough to program your mind for success. You need the skills. I've seen public speakers who love the spotlight and the sound of their own voice. But confidence alone won't do it. These entrepreneurs are bloviators, boring everybody at networking meetings. Skilled speakers get to the point and keep their audience in mind. Being skilled means having prepared speeches.

There are at least three speeches entrepreneurs need to master: the elevator speech, the sales presentation, and the signature speech.

Let's start with the **elevator speech.** The name comes from the idea that if you got into an elevator and your ideal decision maker was there, you would have about 30 seconds to introduce yourself before arriving at the next floor. Too often business owners show up without preparing for a networking meeting. If you've ever scratched your head with confusion after hearing an introduction, that's a person who's unprepared. Three common elevator pitch mistakes are:

1. Too long
2. Not clear
3. All about them

Nobody wants to listen to a person drone on for three minutes when there's a roomful of people. Save that for one-on-one meetings and get to the point. Prepare a 15-second, 30-second- and one-minute version. Then take your cue from the facilitator. Even more effective, is to have a one-sentence elevator pitch. Some one-liners include: *I help speakers book more business. I help companies sell more in less time. I work with people who want to start a business and grow a business.*

If your message is unclear, you will not attract prospects. People won't refer you. You won't be memorable. Brevity enhances clarity. Don't mention everything you do. Keep the message high level. Start with one standalone sentence. Then add more details. Test it with people you don't know and then ask them to explain what you do. You may be surprised.

Another mistake is making the pitch all about you. Nobody cares about your products and services. They're interested in what you can do for them. So, include a benefit and show how you're unique. Rather than saying how you're better, instead say, "How we're different is..." When giving an elevator pitch, tailor it to the audience and remember the 4 Cs.- Clear, Concise, Confident, Compelling.

The second speech entrepreneurs need is the **sales presentation**. This is different from an elevator pitch, which is an introduction. It's often delivered as a webinar or in-person meeting. This requires a special blend of selling and providing value. A good rule of thumb is spending the bulk of the presentation describing the prospect's problem. This demonstrates that you understand them and their industry, and you want to address their pain points. Then give them three tips. Don't give away the store. Give them tips they can apply but that don't completely solve their problem. The goal is for them to hire you. Show them how you've helped other clients like them. The final phase is the call to action. Make them an irresistible offer. Close the presentation with a complimentary eBook, checklist, or something they can use. The purpose is to get their email and continue to market to them.

The third speech is the **signature speech.** When an opportunity arises to speak at a conference, you want to be ready. Your signature speech can be a keynote, general session, or concurrent session. By having a ready-made speech, you can use it repeatedly with a little tailoring. Speaking at conferences is a good way to establish your brand and build your business. The signature speech is not a sales pitch. It must be content rich, showcasing your expertise with some entertainment and interaction thrown in. Create a single theme and no more than three key messages. Aim for edutainment. Leave the audience better informed and feeling good. When the signature speech is well-delivered, you'll be invited to more speaking engagements and more business opportunities.

Once you create these three must-have speeches, there'll be other opportunities such as panel presentations and podcast interviews. Starting a podcast is a great marketing strategy, but it also takes a lot of work. An easier option is to be a guest on podcast interviews. You can do that by hiring a company that books guests on podcasts or you can do the research and book yourself. The advantage of podcasts is you can do them anywhere. A good host will promote your company and products and will give you the link to post on social media. Most guest spots are free, so this a powerful way to market. Beware that the same speaking skills apply. Entrepreneurs may forget that this is still a presentation. The most boring podcasts are where two people have a rambling conversation and make inside jokes and references. Always ask about the audience demographics and speak to them.

Not all podcasts will be a fit. Start out with low-risk podcasts where there isn't a big following. Once you feel confident, contact higher level hosts. Prepare for a podcast the way you would prepare for a presentation. Know your goal. Do you want to sell your book? Do you want them to visit your website? Attend your live event? To be a great guest, start with a hook or compelling statement at the opening of the interview. Have three message points that you can continually reference. Tell short, interesting stories and give examples that provide value. Listeners should see themselves in your stories. And always have a call to action. Give them a free download and capture their email. Don't forget to thank the host and refer other guests. Once you have the link, you can place the recording on social media, on your website, and transcribe the audio as a written document.

And now a word about the virtual world. Entrepreneurs must master virtual presentations. They are here to stay. Even when opportunities for in-person speaking abound, there will still be hybrid presentations. Many audiences want to dial in remotely, even to in-person events.

Virtual presentations are challenging. Screen presence is different from stage presence. In 2020 when most people were communicating remotely, I saw a senator dial into a national TV news program from her laptop. She had been a guest many times and was experienced and media savvy. What I saw was the side of her face and she was looking down. I was shocked!

When speaking virtually, know your platform. The top choices are Zoom, Teams, WebEx, and Google Hangouts. Ask the host about their platform and if they have a producer. A producer handles the backend so you can be free to deliver your presentation. You'll need good lighting and sound. Do not speak to the computer without amplification. It will sound tinny. At the very least, wear earbuds or a headset to achieve good sound quality. Sound is more important than light. Your background is also important. If you're on the road and presenting from a hotel room, don't show the bed. Use a green screen and a branded background. You can make your own using www.canva.com. Or you can download many of the backgrounds provided by the platform.

The most challenging skill for presenters is eye contact. Virtual eye contact is different. Don't look at the audience. Look at the lens. Think of yourself as a broadcaster giving a satellite interview. It takes practice. When you're speaking look at the lens. When the audience is speaking, look at them to see their non-verbal communication.

Another distinction is the talking head is dead. Lecturing won't work for virtual presentations. You must break up the message with interactive activities. It's too easy for people to shut off their cameras and multitask. So, get them involved from the get-go.

You can start with a poll. By involving the audience early in the presentation, you're setting your expectations. In addition to polls, you can create small groups with breakout rooms. Ask them to use the Raise Hand icon or they can physically raise their hands in response to questions. Make generous use of the chat. To save time, tell them to type Y for Yes and N for No. At intervals, ask the producer to read questions from the chat and answer them during your presentation.

The most successful virtual presenters intersperse their presentation with interaction. If you're using slides, use simple graphics and limit the number of words. Steve Jobs would give a presentation with one slide of an iPhone. Don't be a voice in a black hole. Unshare the slides from time-to -time in order to speak directly to the audience. Call on individuals and ask them to unmute their microphones. In smaller groups, facilitate a short discussion. If the audience is involved, they will stay attentive.

Entrepreneurs, business owners, and solopreneurs can't compete with large expensive media campaigns. But public speaking is the competitive edge. Combined with social media, public speaking can establish your brand, position your message, and build your business. Public speaking is a powerful and cost-effective marketing strategy. When entrepreneurs invest and have the right mindset and skill set, they can achieve anything. And public speaking will help you get there.

Diane DiResta, CSP, is Founder and CEO of DiResta Communications, Inc., a New York City consultancy serving business leaders who deliver high stakes presentations—whether one-to-one, in front of a crowd or from an electronic platform.   DiResta is the author of *Knockout Presentations: How to Deliver Your Message with Power, Punch, and Pizzazz*, an Amazon.com category best-seller and has spoken on 4 continents. She has unique ability to get to the core of the message and translate complexity into simplicity.

Diane is Past President of the NYC chapter of National Speakers Association and former media trainer for the NBA and WNBA. She was featured on CNN, and quoted in the NY Times, Wall Street Journal, London Guardian, and Investors Business Daily and Bloomberg radio.

Diane is a Certified Speaking Professional, a designation held by less than 12% of speakers nationwide as well as a certified virtual presenter. Her blog, Knockout Presentations, made the Top 50 Public Speaking blogs. And her Linkedin course-Speaking Confidently and Effectively ranked #5 on the Top 20 Most Popular courses.

The Importance of Prenups & Postnups

Arthur D. Ettinger

Prenuptial Agreement Advice & Steps

What are the circumstances that would make a prenup most useful – in what kinds of situations would an individual want to consider a prenup, and those when a prenup isn't necessary?

The most useful aspect of a prenuptial agreement is that it frames and narrows the issues in the event of divorce. We all know that divorce is not cheap, and fees will mount quickly if litigation ensues. A good prenuptial agreement can limit the costs attenuated to the divorce by crystalizing how the financial aspects will be resolved if the marriage goes sideways.

. . .

Also, a prenup is extremely useful and warranted in second marriages and beyond, especially when there are children from a previous relationship. It only makes sense that a parent would want to protect the assets and the interests of children they had before finding love again. Instead of having the law decide, future spouses can chart their own course with a well drafted prenuptial agreement. This doesn't necessarily mean a spouse is cutting their newlywed off, but rather taking the reigns and deciding exactly how their pre-marital and marital estate will be divided, instead of having a stranger in a robe decide. Other strong candidates for a prenup include spouses with significant assets, including business interests which will likely appreciate resulting from active efforts by the owner spouse, and those individuals anticipating significant inheritances in the future. While inheritances are already protected, a prenuptial agreement will make it crystal clear, and parties will be able to avoid the financial and emotional burden of prolonged discovery battles in divorce court.

There are other factors that make a prenuptial agreement useful. For example, where the parties live may affect how assets and liabilities are treated. In community property states such as Washington or California, marital property is divided equally. Also, a spouse may be on the hook for the other's incurred liabilities. A properly drafted prenup by an experienced family law attorney can safeguard and protect against such events.

That's not to say that a prenuptial agreement is for everyone. Individuals getting married for the first time with limited assets and little or no debt, with similar income/earning potential, are not typically raising the prenup conversation. Nonetheless, there is a common misconception that prenuptial agreement are only useful for the wealthy. Just because you may not have much at the time of marriage, that does not mean that is where you will find yourself in the future.

Some will often say that a prenup takes the romance out of the relationship. While I understand and appreciate why, I don't agree. Marriage is about communication. Money is one of the top reasons marriages fail. Couples need to open the dialogue before they are married on how financial decisions will be made. A prenup is a good way to start that conversation. If the relationship is solid, with healthy and productive communication, no prenup will erode the romance.

Prenup vs. Postnup? Why would or should a couple wait until after their marriage to create the agreement?

Postnuptial agreements are less common than prenuptial agreements but are becoming more popular. Spouses might wait until after their marriage to create a postnuptial agreement for a variety of reasons or even because they wish they had made a prenuptial agreement from the outset. A postnuptial agreement can also modify terms in a previously executed prenuptial agreement.

If a couple has a significant change in finances or are having marital issues, a postnuptial agreement can be useful to reflect changed circumstances. Postnups can address and establish plans in case of divorce, separation, or death in the same way prenuptial agreements do.

Common Steps to Get a Prenup

1. COMMUNCIATE EARLY. I encourage my clients to have a candid conversation with their future spouse about getting a prenuptial agreement as soon as possible. Don't spring the conversation on them suddenly. Set a time to sit down and discuss together.

2. CONSULT AND RETAIN AN EXPERIECED FAMILY LAW ATTORNEY. Find and retain an attorney who has experience in prenuptial agreements. While your business lawyer or family member might be great, prenuptial agreements are a niche area of law best handled by a family law attorney or even a trusts and estates experienced with prenuptial agreements.

3. GATHER YOUR DOCUMENTS. When a potential client first contacts me about a prenup, I'm candid with them from the start. I want to know as much as I can about their financials and those of their fiancé, including assets, liabilities, and respective incomes. At this point, I will ask clients to put together a summary of their assets and liabilities and to provide copies of tax returns. Not only is this vital to properly advise the client and determine what

should go into the document, but it is also necessary to exchange with the client's fiancé and counsel. A key component of a well drafted prenuptial agreement is full financial disclosure. Prenups devoid of financial disclosure, albeit minimal, will likely be declared invalid if scrutinized down the road.

4. DETERMINE WHAT WILL BE INCLUDED. Once the financials are clear, and the client's wishes are clear, we then discuss what terms and provisions will be included. Not everybody wants to provide for every detail. For example, a spouse may only want to address the disposition of a home in the prenup. Often, these discussions may be with other individuals, along with the client, such as family members, accountants or financial advisors.

5. DRAFT AND NEGOTIATE THE PRENUPTIAL AGREEMENT. Sometimes the document is drafted first. Sometimes the terms are first negotiated and agreed upon and then the document is drafted. Either way, both parties should be represented by independent counsel.

6. CAREFULLY REVIEW THE DOCUMENT. The client needs to see every draft and redraft of the agreement. This sounds like common sense, right? I cannot tell you how many times I have heard in the middle of a divorce that involved a prenup and one party, either my client or the other side, says they never reviewed the prenuptial agreement before signing it. The document is going to have lasting effects for many

years to come; it is worth reviewing before putting your signature on it.

7. PROPERLY EXECUTED. When the prenuptial agreement is finalized with terms agreeable to both parties, it is time for the document to be signed and properly notarized. Some practitioners also video record the execution of the prenuptial agreement. While I do not do this in every single instance, I almost always have the parties to the documents sign affidavits to prevent them from trying to set it aside in the future. Also, while not necessarily fatal, it's best to avoid the situation where the agreement is signed on the eve of the wedding day.

Arthur Ettinger is a Partner & Chair, NY Matrimonial & Family Law Dept. at GreenspoonMarder. He represents and advises clients in all aspects of matrimonial and family law, including negotiating and drafting pre and post nuptial agreements and separation agreements and litigating child custody and complex economic issues throughout New York State.

He also represents MLB players in their contract negotiations.

Leading With Effective Communication
By Mike Greenly

W ould you like an even more successful career?

I'd never have risen the corporate ladder if I hadn't learned how to convey my thoughts effectively in both written and spoken form, including overcoming "stage fright."

For any leader today, being able to communicate effectively is *more* important than ever, given that humans now pay *less* attention to input than our species ever has. That statement is not hyperbolic. As revealed in a 2015 study by Microsoft:

- Average attention span of a goldfish: 9 seconds
- Average human attention span in 2001: 12 seconds
- Average human attention span in 2015: 8.25 seconds and headed South.

My goal here is to reward *your* attention by sharing a few of the insights I use when helping my clients communicate with impact and memorability. Let's start with some secrets of writing an effective speech or presentation, regardless of format. Then I'll share a few tips on presenting with impact before a live audience.

First: determine your concise take-away message

The most common communications mistake I observe across the board – in speeches, PowerPoints, business memos, corporate videos, etc. – is trying to convey too many points at once. These days more than ever, a scattershot approach is not effective.

If you jam too many thoughts into a single communication or visual, your message will likely not stick. Organize your writing around a single, overall message – a communications "North Star" – and your big picture point will be better remembered.

It's also true – as the saying goes – that we get one chance to make a first impression. Start with something relevant to your audience. The first sentence of this chapter was intended to get your attention up front by offering you a "What's In it For Me," otherwise known as "WIIFM."

Take maximum advantage of the Internet

A few decades ago, I'd traipse over to the Barnes & Noble bookstore in Manhattan – buying books as "research" for whatever I needed to write. I'm no expert in sports, art history, automobiles, or many other subjects, but some of my clients are. They appreciate analogies in subjects they care

Leading With Effective Communication   21

about and relate to. These days, my fingers do the walking straight to Google.

You many think everyone knows about Google, but many people still don't get how versatile a helper it can be. On a cold winter's day during COVID in New York City, I heard a neighbor in my building's lobby complaining about having his glasses fog up while wearing a mask. He was grateful when I told him that all he had to do was to ask Google:

How do I stop my glasses from fogging up when wearing a mask?

(I did that just now and got over a million hits!)

You can ask Google: How to write an awards acceptance speech? How to make my PowerPoint more interesting, etc., etc. The Internet is a richer source of help than some of us realize.

The writer's paradox: it takes longer to write shorter

You MUST be willing to step back and have a fresh read of your own writing. Critique yourself ruthlessly and make edits as you notice needs. Yes, the process of re-reading takes a bit more time, but emerging from the editing weeds for a "fresh" overall look can cause you to see improvements you might have missed. That little extra bit of time can pay off!

Use Emphasis Words when writing something to be heard

When writing a speech, PowerPoint, or any presentation you'll deliver aloud, you must HEAR it (not just in your head) in order to properly evaluate it.

I use a specific technique I call *Emphasis Words* when I write a speech. It's proven helpful to many of my clients. I capitalize Key Words to encourage the speaker to "hit" them with extra oomph in delivering a message aloud.

Try saying the following sentences aloud ... each time "hitting" with extra emphasis the word I've put into bold capital letters. (In the first sentence, "I" is the emphasized word.) Notice how the vocal emphasis affects the resulting meaning.

I didn't drive our car yesterday. (Someone else did.)

I **DIDN'T** drive our car yesterday. (I'm INSISTING that I didn't)

I didn't **DRIVE** our car yesterday. (I just SAT in it and read.)

I didn't drive **OUR** car yesterday. (I drove someone else's.)

I didn't drive our **CAR** yesterday. (I drove our truck.)

I didn't drive our car **YESTERDAY** (I drove it the day before that.)

If you're writing a presentation, it will take extra time to "hear" yourself aloud. But I promise you: the result will be better if you do.

Those are just a few tips I've learned about writing/creating a message. But how about delivering it?

COVID has – for now – limited the in-person meetings and events that used to be an ongoing part of corporate life, not to mention the closed Broadway theaters as I type these words. I'm assuming, however, that we'll eventually get back to face-to-face presentations, notwithstanding how important Zoom has become in the time of coronavirus. So here's a bit of what I've learned about overcoming "stage fright" with tips I've used to help my clients improve their skills.

First – how do you, yourself, feel about standing on a stage, looking out at a crowd and delivering your thoughts to everyone staring back? For the first decades of my life, that was impossible without feeling sick to my stomach.

There is a name for the dread of public speaking: "glossophobia." I've known for decades about surveys showing that many people fear an audience more than they dread heights, darkness, death or, in my case, the dentist's drill.

Having had extreme "stage fright" for years, I changed in a big way after some transformational experiences. Not only did I learn to hold the attention of an audience – even as large as 5,000 people. Also, to my surprise, I actually learned to enjoy it!

Leadership, in my opinion, *requires* the ability to present one's ideas effectively to others. How you communicate affects the way you're perceived, whether as a *thought* leader or in leading a team, department, or entire organization.

Be Yourself, Only Bigger and Better On-Stage

The *single* most important lesson I've learned – and I'll share how I learned it – is to harness your authenticity when delivering a speech or presentation. That realization has made a tremendous difference for me and then for many of my clients. Helping people learn to be their best selves onstage, while also being their *real* selves (thereby making a more genuine connection with an audience) is satisfying ... especially for me, because that ability used to feel hopelessly out of reach.

I didn't start out in life with confidence at all. I grew up in Beaufort, SC – a small, beautiful island community next to the Atlantic. My challenge was being woefully "different," which affected my self-esteem. I was "the Dirty Jew Boy" in a largely Southern Baptist town. Trust me: It doesn't build a boy's self-image to have swastikas and hate words carved into his school locker.

To make things worse, I was asked to skip the second grade. (I'd been finishing the classwork too soon and becoming restless.) Now I was even more different: a year younger than all my classmates.

Decades later – after tons of psychotherapy and even some training as a "shrink" – I had risen in corporate life. At one point, I led the development of 300 new products a year at Avon. Then I published the vitally important sales brochure, 22 million copies every two weeks. And finally, I was in charge of all meetings and events: that meant I had to learn to give a speech on-stage to an audience of thousands. (Gulp!)

I was whisked up to the executive floor and given a lavish budget to redecorate the office to my taste – one of the perks of being an Avon VP back then. But old insecurities haunted me. They were amplified by the presence of an established VP down the hall who soon began to feel like a rival, a competitor in what was supposed to be a united team of Officers Together.

I'll call him Big Guy, since if he wasn't precisely 6'8", he was nonetheless an unusually tall and towering man with a huge and overwhelming personality. He was the extrovert's extrovert, fearless in displaying his (undeniable) creativity and charisma. He was in charge of sales promotion to consumers while I was now in charge of field communications. You know: with actual live *people* for whom you have to get up on-stage and speak, nervous or not.

Among my other roles, I led the August Conference – the annual sales meeting for District Sales Managers flown in from around the country. By the time they headed back home, they had to be pumped up with enthusiasm and "belief," ready to ignite passion within the hundreds of reps they each managed locally.

So Big Guy and I would both need to be on-stage during the same meeting. We'd be observed and – inescapably – compared to each other.

The familiar dread of public speaking came back to haunt me, as I started planning the Conference and my remarks. What a timid little mouse I would surely seem in contrast to Big Guy. The more I realized that I could never be like him – that I would fail if I tried – the more miserable I became.

Until it clicked in my brain that, instead of trying to be a pale imagination of Big Guy, what I actually needed to be was the best version of *myself.*

Off-stage I'm his opposite. It's simply not within me to bully or badger someone to achieve my goals, nor to be strident or flamboyant. A friend named me years ago, "the most earnest person on the Eastern Seaboard" – intensely sincere, but much too polite and empathetic to overwhelm others, even as a negotiating technique.

Of course, my rival's style worked beautifully for him. I'd witnessed how brilliantly dynamic he was on-stage. But as with shoes that don't fit, I suddenly understood that his way of presenting would be awkward and uncomfortable for me as the person I am.

That fundamental idea – being true to one's self instead of straining to be a pale imitation of someone else or some "image" in one's brain – is stupidly simple and obvious now. But what a difference it made when I applied it!

When it was time for my motivational message -- my turn to inspire -- I didn't try to be flashy like my colleague. Instead, I addressed the audience in a simple and personal way.

I recalled my first week with the company – when Avon had sent me to Iowa to see what "direct selling" was really like. That week out in the Heartland had a profound effect on me.

I was required on the first day to go door-to-door selling in an actual territory. It was humiliating. The whole day I sold one nail polish.

The next day, I told my audience, I accompanied the best sales rep in the territory. I got to see how personal door-to-door selling was actually to be done. This friendly, down-to-earth woman had real relationships with her customers; they depended on her and clearly liked her. She was one of the best sales reps in the state.

When I marveled afterward at how effective this woman was, she gave credit to her District Sales Manager, the very people who'd be my audience years later at the August Conference. That experience with the rep helped me appreciate the phenomenal impact that local district leadership had, not just on our sales but on our sales*people.*

The most pivotal change in her life, she said – as her comments moved and excited me about the company I'd just joined – was the self-esteem she had gained for herself. She directly attributed her newfound pride and happiness to her supportive Manager.

While sharing this story on-stage with my sales management audience, I did not gallivant across the space trying to simulate the extroverted "showman" I'll never be. Instead I consciously allowed myself to get back in touch with the real emotion I had felt in discovering how my new company had enhanced an Iowa housewife's life, thanks to the training and guidance of her Manager.

As I recalled and (importantly) re-*experienced* those feelings under the spotlight, while praising my sales management audience for the daily impact they had on the lives of those they led, I heard sniffles and occasional sobs echoing around the giant hotel ballroom. I knew beyond doubt that I was having a significant impact on my audience, simply by being me--sincere, earnest and emotional.

Afterward, countless attendees came up to grasp my hands or give me hugs. Over and over they said: "one of the best speeches ever!" That crucial lesson, about the power of being true to one's essence, has been incredibly useful ever since, both on and off stage.

When I write speeches for executives these days, that insight helps me live up to the slogan I developed for my Internet ads: "Sound like yourself ... only better." And when I coach executives – many of whom are secretly as nervous as I used to be -- I draw on my story to help them find new poise and security as they speak.

This is just a single chapter, not an in-person session. But let me quickly offer a few additional (important) things I've learned.

Movement On-Stage

I now know never to be one of those speakers who "wander," tracing a restless path across the stage as they talk.

If you don't know this yet, I promise: you will be more effective and convincing if you plant yourself on-stage like a steadfast pillar of authority, the Tree of Knowledge. Move across the stage only when there's an important new point to be made, or a change in mood. Then *re*-plant yourself in your new location.

It doesn't matter if this feels artificial to you at first. After all, you're giving a "performance." That's not about being real ... just making it feel that way to the audience. I'll say more about this in a bit.

Hand Gestures

The best advice is the simplest: give yourself permission to be you. If you talk with your hands naturally, then do! If you don't use your hands in "real life," don't try to fake it on-stage.

Audiences crave a connection with anyone addressing them. Otherwise, you just become part of a "show" — including your gestures – without having created real engagement with your listeners.

So in whatever way your hands move (or don't) when you're expressing your own message, that's how your hands should be on-stage.

The most important guidance is to let your mind and voice be in sync with your words. If you feel – not just think, but feel — the meaning of your words when you say them ... your audience will feel them, too. They'll sense and believe in your genuineness as you allow yourself to experience your own message, first in every rehearsal and then actually on-stage.

The Right Kind of Rehearsal

One imperative I've learned, which many presenters underestimate, is the importance of the right kind of rehearsal, both quantity and quality.

Quantity

You want to rehearse your text so often that you know the material well enough to be comfortable and un-strained, able to look up from the page if you're presenting from paper at a lectern, able to finish a sentence or thought before looking down for the next cue.

This is not the same as "memorizing" a word-for-word script. I recommend against that. Having to rely solely on memory puts tremendous pressure on a speaker and requires a greater investment in time and technique for natural, relaxed delivery.

There are separate tips for working from a TelePrompter, but this space isn't big enough for every piece of advice. But the next tip – about "quality" of rehearsal – applies to *every* presentation you'll ever give, regardless of format.

Quality

The way you rehearse can make a surprising difference during your ultimate presentation.

Of much greater consequence than the number of times you rehearse is how you do it: Quality more than Quantity. The more mentally "real" you can make each run-through, the more confident and effective you'll be in front of your audience.

Forget forever about reviewing the words of your speech in silence. *No!* That misses the point. Making rehearsal real means actively imagining everyone in front of you – each time you rehearse – and always addressing them with the same energy you expect to use on-stage.

So rehearse *aloud*, including imaginary eye contact with your pretend audience. (Good quality rehearsal is fatiguing – like a real presentation.)

The right kind of rehearsal also means being as conscious of your pacing and variety as you would want to be in front of in-person listeners. Again: each time you rehearse! Making every rehearsal as much like "the real thing" as you can, will pay off in your eventual delivery.

The paradox of being effective in delivering a speech is learning to be authentic on the one hand, while always remembering that a speech is also a "performance." It's both real and artificial, at once.

It takes focus, energy and the right kind of rehearsal to effectively project yourself as you speak. Many speakers write notes to themselves in their texts: reminders during delivery to SMILE … show ENERGY … be FRIENDLY, etc.

You need to be a "bigger" version of yourself in front of hundreds of people or more. It will not work to address an audience the same way you might chat with a friend over coffee. The physical gap between you and your audience is psychological, too. Your listeners won't be aware of it, but that separation affects their ability to maximally "connect" with you.

The literal gap is about height (you're standing, they're sitting) and distance (between the front row and where you stand). To overcome it requires most presenters to be more energized, with more presence, than they ever would be off-stage. You want each member of the audience to feel as though you're talking to and connecting directly and personally with them, regardless of how far away you actually are.

It can require a change of one's mindset to be one's own authentic self – while, paradoxically, being better and bigger on stage at the same time. But the core truth in everything I use in coaching my clients, is the one that changed me and my life: drawing on and making the most of the inherent power of who I am, never trying to be an imitation of someone else, no matter how effective that other person might appear to be.

So when you're faced with the challenge of giving a speech, no matter how tense or fretful you feel, take stock of who are. For real. Connect to the truth at the heart of your personal brand. Be in touch with your genuine essence as you speak.

As I've mentioned, there are a number of "tips" that can help one be more effective. But the single most important technique is that simple but essential mindset – finding the courage to be your own real self (only "bigger") when you're on-stage.

I can tell you this with certainty: it is possible to make that change. And it's very satisfying when you do. It can make all the difference in enabling you to hear one of the sweetest sounds on earth: the applause that you have earned for who you actually are.

Bottom line: effective communication – written and/or spoken – makes for more successful leadership. And will give you more pleasure as you lead!

Mike Greenly's corporate career includes educational publishing at Scholastic, Inc. and consumer marketing at Lever Brothers. Ultimately, he became the youngest VP in the history of Avon Products, the world's #1 Direct Seller at the time.

Today as Mike Greenly Marketing, Inc., he uses his gift for words to help execs and their teams as a writer (speeches, PowerPoints, videos, ghostwriting, etc.), speech coach, and motivational speaker. He's a published author and lyricist (his "Our Great Virginia" became the state's anthem in 2015.)

Although he often creates desired messages from scratch, he's never met a client's first draft he can't improve to their delight.

www.mikegreenly.com greenlypro@mikegreenly.com

What Entrepreneurs can learn from The Rolling Stones
Robert Intelisano

Rolling Stones, Rolling in Dollars!

Last week, I had the pleasure and privilege of flying to Pittsburgh, PA. to see the Rolling Stones play an outdoor concert at Heinz Field, home of the Pittsburgh Steelers! I flew from LaGuardia to Pittsburgh (a 1-hour fight) and my best friend Jay, from Lehigh University (who lives in Bel Air, Maryland) picked me up at the airport and we drove to center city Pittsburgh for a 2-night stay.

This was not an everyday show, as the Stones have been jamming for almost 60 years. One of my favorite Rock bands, I have seen The Stones opening their 1989 Steel Wheels tour in Philadelphia, at the MGM Grand Hotel in Las Vegas, and also in 1994 Toronto to name a few. That 1989 tour is when the Stones changed what was a typical stadium tour into a theatre-like setting with huge blow-up dolls while playing "Honky Tonk Woman!"

Other than perhaps Kiss, the Rolling Stones have mastered the marketing of their brand and logo, the famous Big Red Lips and Tongue. For Mick Jagger and the Rolling Stones, Rock and Roll is BIG Business!

The Stones had last played Heinz Field in 2015. The total capacity of Heinz Field is 68,000, although they do block off about 15,000 seats behind the stage. Their revenue from that 2015 Pittsburgh show was $9,000,000 from the 50,000+ fans that attended.

Mick Jagger, arguably the best front man in history, is, in my opinion, what makes the Rolling Stones different from all other bands. Few people know that Mick spent some of his teenage years studying Finance and Economics at the prestigious London School of Economics, before quitting school to start a band!

Most bands concentrate on their craft and leave the day-to-day business operations to their agents. Not 78-year-old Mick, whose net worth is over $360 million. The Rolling Stones operate like a well-oiled business with 300 employees. It costs them $1,000,000 per week to "keep the show on the road!" They had 11 people on stage and many more behind the scenes. In a 1994 interview with Ed Bradley of 60 minutes, (the 14-minute interview can be seen on YouTube) Mick referred to himself as the Chief Executive of Business Operations of a Mobile Virtual Corporation.

Here are 5 surprising lessons business owners can learn from Mick Jagger:

1. It is Not Enough to Have a Great Idea or Product: There have been many great bands over the years; however, only a few have ALL members financially secure for life. It takes business skill to know what gigs to book, how to promote new albums, how much to charge for tickets, and how to manage employees.

2. Learn from Your Mistakes: The Stones lost big money in the 1960's. Jagger was quoted in a 2002 Fortune Magazine article saying, "I'll never forget the deals I did in the 60's, which were just terrible. You say, oh, I'm a creative person, I won't worry about this. But that just doesn't work!"

3. Do NOT Give Up: The Stones song "You Can't Always Get What You Want" carries a message for small business owners. "You can't always get what you want, but if you try sometimes, you might just find, you get what you need!"

4. Stay Relevant: One of the reasons the Stones have had staying power through generations is because they keep people talking. Whether putting out new albums, licensing their old songs to new movies, the Stones continue to be a topic of conversation.

. . .

5. Understand the Importance of Collaboration: Jagger has made many savvy decisions about partners. Two band members (until drummer Charlie Watts recently passed away) have been with him since the 1960's. Others have shuttled through the band over the years. It is important to know when to make changes for the betterment of the band.

Mick Jagger and the Rolling Stones have lived long and storied lives. Since Mick has 8 children with 5 women, it is good that he has been prudent with his money. He made a excellent career choice, and when you do what you love, work will never be a chore! Rock On Rolling Stones!

Robert C. Intelisano, CSA, CLU, LUTCF

As the President of Intelisano & Associates, Inc. Robert quarterbacks an experienced team of independent professionals who help Law and CPA firm clients with creative solutions using insurance-based protection products. Areas of concentration include:

• Life Insurance Case Analysis Review and Design

• Estate Planning and Premium Financing for the Affluent

• Licensed Life Insurance Settlement Broker

• Health Care and Employee Benefits

• Experienced Court Liaison

Ignite your business ... write a book!

Stephanie Larkin

What can help you to stand out from your competition in a crowded field?
What gives you instant credibility—even when you aren't in the room?
What can streamline your in-house processes and save money?
What can enhance your workshops and training sessions?
What can you hand to a prospective client to close the deal?

The answer to these and many other questions is . . . **A BOOK!**

A book can close deals with prospective clients, illuminate others to your core mission, save money by clarifying business systems, act as the ultimate sales rep who even goes home with your prospects, and give your resume an unprecedented boost.

According to the Small Business Association, over 625,000 new businesses open each year. Those new, enthusiastic business owners—together with the existing businesses—form a lot of competition if you want to get your business seen, remembered, and respected in such a crowded marketplace. Building your market is all about exposure and perception— people must be made aware of you and your business, and then they must have a positive impression in order to want to work with you. Writing a book helps by setting you apart from your competitors while establishing your credibility in the field—a win-win!

Consider the following scenario—we've all been there before!

The murmur of chatter permeates the room as people stream into the auditorium for the morning's presentations. Admittedly, some participants are anxiously awaiting the day's events, while others—more skeptical types—have more of an "I dare you to impress me!" attitude as they trudge into the auditorium.

Julie has been to many, many such events in her work life, and would much rather be at her desk catching up on work than hearing the morning's panel of speakers. She takes her seat with little expectation of learning anything from the speakers and opens the program to see just what she is in for this morning. Scanning down the list of names, she isn't familiar with any, but her eye catches one in particular—Amanda Grey, author of "Recharge Your Life and Work with _____ ." Suddenly Julie perks up, interested in learning more about what this expert has to say.

There is no doubt about it—having a book "to your name" sets you apart in a way like no other. In fact, once you have written a book, you will find that it is so critical to your professional persona that the words "author of _____" will appear right after your name—before any other credentials.

> *"Most people believe almost anything they see in print."*
> ~ E.B. White, Charlotte's Web

But I Can't Write a Book!

There are as many different ways of writing a book as there are books in the world, and truly no "right" or "wrong" way, as long as it gets done. Before we get into tips, structures, and strategies on writing the book, the first decision is who is actually going to do the writing. You may already be aware that not all books are written by the person whose name is on the cover, so there is definitely some grey area here with deciding who will write your book. Your options in general are:

You Write Your Own Book

I particularly love this option, as the pride in completing such an endeavor far outweighs the time, effort, and learning curve involved. I have personally coached many prospective authors through the writing of their book, and there is nothing quite like the feeling of seeing your name on the cover of a book—wow!

Writing a book yourself can also be a great way to test the waters in a new field, develop ideas about a particular industry or even learn more about yourself. You can write a book alone or utilize the services of a coach, beta readers, and editor or even writing group to help refine your message and keep you accountable to finishing the task. And while writing a book is certainly not easy, 90% of people polled say that writing a book is a major life goal, so you will be fulfilling a dream for millions of others with your book.

You have a team approach to your book

Many books are written by a team, whether it is obvious as in a compilation of stories/articles, or less pronounced, such as many of our most popular fiction writers. Team or not, the author's name is on the cover, so before you ask, yes, you get "credit" for writing the book!

Writing a book with others is a fantastic way to get things done, especially when it comes to books written to streamline business practices, use in workshops, or other money-saving ideas. Team approaches help books come together quickly, and with a team, there are more stakeholders who have a vested interest in the success of the book. There could be one on-site team member who is the gatekeeper/editor (that could also be you, as author), or another editor/ghostwriter off-site can coordinate the team and their submissions. I have worked with many compilations, and it is exciting to see the book come together with many people involved in its ultimate success.

. . .

You hire a ghostwriter

I love the term "ghostwriter"—it conjures up all sorts of fantastic images in my head. And since I have ghostwritten many books, I have a keen desire to keep a white sheet in my office to pull over my head when I need inspiration.

Seriously speaking though, hiring a ghostwriter doesn't mean that you will have no input into the creative process at all. Quite the contrary--a ghostwriter for the types of non-fiction books we are discussing should be gathering information, conducting interviews, and learning about exactly what needs to be written in the book. In the case of utilizing a ghostwriter for manuals and other in-house books, a ghostwriter can be considered a "contracted consultant" who visits your place of business and works with your staff to develop the best possible book to streamline processes and save you time and money. All of that and you don't need to type a word—a pretty good deal for all!

You may also opt for something "in-between", like writing a rough draft yourself and having a writer flesh it out from there or other variations. Your options are endless, and you needn't let the HOW get in the way of the final goal—a book to benefit your business!

5 Book "types" so easy - they practically write themselves!

There are as many ways to organize the content in a book as there are books in the world, and with over 4,000 new books being added to Amazon every day, that's a lot of books! Here are 5 book types which you may not have considered, which are MUCH easier than the traditional "start at the beginning and write until the end" approach..

Book Type #1 - the book of ideas/tips
Examples:
25 Biblical Laws of Success
17 Indisputable Laws of Teamwork

If you go to Amazon and simply type "50 ways to ___ " you will hit upon a jackpot of book titles. Whether you go with 50 or 5, books set up in this manner are a breeze to write, set you up as an approachable "expert" in your field, and are enticing to read, as the reader feels as if they are going to glean tangible, applicable tips in a hurry.

Book Type #2 - the book of questions
Examples:
100 Questions Every First-Time Home Buyer Should Ask
101 Questions to Ask Before You Get Engaged

Whether you are in finance or personal growth, I am sure that you ask your clients a lot of questions - in some fields, the questions sum up a majority of what you do! And whether your questions are designed to lead your reader to further introspection or simply to record information, your primary goal of leading readers to YOU and the positives of working with you will be realized. A book of questions contains a lot of blank spaces and can be written rather easily, as you know best the questions your customers are asking.

Book Type #3 - case studies/stories
Examples:
Case Studies in Abnormal Psychology
12 Classic Tales from the World of Wall Street
Real Estate Stories: Hilarious & Uncensored Tales From a
Property Management Expert

Books of stories are big hits with readers, and they love to read about others facing the same issues and challenges as themselves yet coming out on top. As a writer, you can either draw upon your own experiences and stories—changing names and identifying information where appropriate—or research biographies or cases related to your target area.

Book Type #4 - compilations
Examples:
Insider Secrets for Small to Medium Business Owners by Top
Business and Marketing Experts
Insights & Innovation From Top Local Business Owners,
Professionals & Community Leaders
The Real Book of Real Estate: Real Experts. Real Stories. Real Life

When in doubt, have other people write your book for you! Not only can a compilation relieve you of the major portion of writing responsibilities but inviting colleagues to partner in your project is a win-win for everyone. You end up with a book, they get exposure, and you gain incredible opportunities to network with others and give them a great opportunity—one which may be repaid to you in the future!

Book Type #5 - how to book
Examples:
How To Pay Off Your Mortgage In 5 Years
How to Read Literature Like a Professor

"How-to" books are such a popular topic area, they even have their own category on Amazon! Some authors worry that writing a how-to book will make people want to "do it themselves" and not enlist your services. On the contrary--a how-to book exhibits your expertise in a particular area. Let's face it - some people like to do things themselves (even things they perhaps shouldn't be doing!), but others like to know a bit of information - just enough to realize that they are in way over their head!

You're on your way! By crystallizing the reason WHY you wish to write your book and HOW you will be able to get moving, you can approach the actual writing with a plan and goal in mind. Like setting out for a road trip, having a map and hotel reservations at your destination ensures that you WILL arrive at the correct place in a timely matter. And just like a road trip, the journey is half the fun!

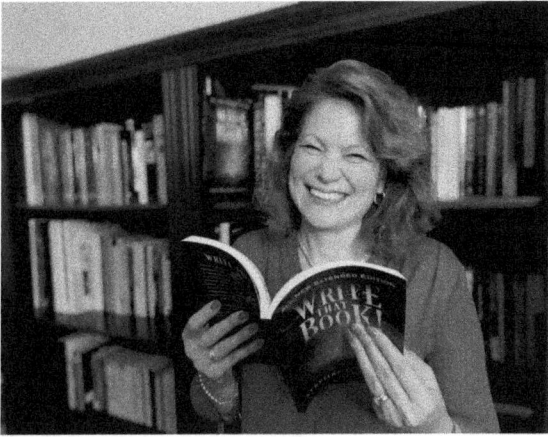

Stephanie Larkin is the founder and president of Red Penguin Books and Web Solutions, a book and web publication company for over 15 years, publishing over 100 books per year of all types and genres, with authors hailing from 6 different continents around the world.

Stephanie is the author of **Build Your Business With Books**, **Write That Book!**, **365 Reasons to Celebrate!** and **SCORE with Social Media**, in addition to many ghostwritten publications. In addition to spearheading Red Penguin Classes - the educational wing of Red Penguin Books offering online classes in writing and book marketing, Stephanie teaches in the Marketing Department at Nassau Community College. Stephanie is the host of television's **Technically Speaking**, an award-winning educational cable TV series airing in Queens and Long Island, **The Author Corner**, airing on Verizon, Optimum and QPTV, as well as the web show **Between the Covers**, and **Once and Future Authors** podcast. Stephanie is the host of a new show - sponsored by the Ahmedabad Book Club in India - featuring writers and book lovers from around the globe launching in 2022. Stephanie's goal and company motto is *"Changing lives ... one book at a time!"*

Write YOUR book - visit RedPenguinBooks.com and get started today!

Networking
Howie Mann

Productive Networking

In sales, a good networker will do very well. An excellent networker will make a fortune. This is true no matter what you are selling, whether it be a product or service, high end or low end, in person or over the phone. But there is also the "good kind" of networking that we are going to discuss, and the "stick your business card down the throat of every person you come in contact with" kind that you should be wary of.

There are so many productive ways to network that meeting new people should never be a problem. Here are just a few suggestions that you can hopefully use or draw inspiration from to find others that might work for you:

Join a business networking organization

BNI

LeTip

Adrian's Network

IBO

Join local clubs or go a step further and become an officer of those clubs

Rotary Club

Kiwanis Club

Knights of Columbus

Elks Lodge

Local Chamber of Commerce

Local Country Club

Become a board member of a local non-profit

YMCA

Salvation Army

Goodwill

Volunteer with a local organization

Your church or synagogue

Leukemia & Lymphoma Society

Habitat For Humanity

Play a sport

Bowling

Softball

Soccer

Golf

Tennis

Keep in mind that these activities can also be integrated with other areas of your life. If you have children, everything that they do can become an opportunity to network, and the best part is that you get to spend more quality time with them while building your business. Some thoughts there are:

Coach their sports team

Join the PTA

Boy Scouts or Girl Scouts

These are not only great ways to just meet other people but also other business people who can be a great source of business or referrals for you and your business. They are also people you can give your business to when in need of their product or service instead of a stranger or large national chain that has no loyalty to you.

But make no mistake, just joining one, or several, of these organizations is not going to rake in the big bucks. What you do once you join is equally important as showing up. A famous comedian, who shall remain nameless, once said, "80% of life is showing up." There is a lot of truth in this, but the other 20% is made up of what we do once we get there.

It is so important to make the most of every opportunity you are given. When asked to lead special events, chair certain committees, or simply take charge of a fundraiser – say yes. This can go a long way to standing out from the others who just show up and affords you the opportunity of being asked again. Sometimes, it only takes one "no" to never be asked again. Taking on positions of leadership offer you more exposure, and in turn, more opportunities to grow your business.

I remember being at the gym this one time, minding my own business on the treadmill, and the guy next to me strikes up a conversation and asks what I do for a living. I could have just kept my head down and focused on the workout, but I chose to engage him in a conversation. Turns out he was in the business of selling postage meters while I was involved with copiers. Our products were complimentary for many of our clients.

It is now years later, and he and I are lifelong networking partners, a "Power Team" if you will. I can introduce him to the decision-makers at the companies I deal with, and he can do the same for me. It's like our books of business instantly doubled.

I had a similar experience while out to the movies with my wife. Now, she will tell you that I just can't help commenting on almost anything with complete strangers. So the guy next to us sits down with fresh popcorn and I mention how good it smells. He was kind enough to offer me some and we struck up a conversation. Turns out he was in the office supply business.

That night another "Power Team" was formed. We have now helped each other with referrals and sales opportunities for the last ten-plus years. The point here isn't that I'm a social butterfly, but that when we ask other people questions about their life and business good things can happen. There is an old expression that conveniently points out how we have two ears but only one mouth for a reason. People prefer to talk about themselves far more than listen to you speak about yours from the moment you meet.

You will eventually get your turn to speak; just be patient. I always start by asking them for a business card first, then carefully looking it over so I can come back to them with an interesting question or two:

How long have you been doing this?

Do you know my friend "name" who also does this?

I may have someone who can use your product or service. What areas do you cover?

. . .

How is business these days?

When is your busiest season?

Is this your own company?

What attracted you to this field?

Who is a good prospect for you?

This can take some time to get comfortable doing, but once you master it, the process is very enjoyable and starts to come naturally. It is also nice when new business starts rolling in, thanks to these new contacts.

Another way of networking is to attend the parties, events, and celebrations that your clients may invite you to. This can be in the form of an anniversary, holiday party, or fundraiser. No matter what it is, the best thing to do is show up. There you can get introduced to their contacts, which will result in even more business. If it is a fundraiser, be sure to donate something. Items that have your company information on them and can be raffled are a great choice because you are remembered long after the event.

Networking anywhere and everywhere will make you more successful than you ever thought. One example of this is an airport. They are notorious for leaving way too much downtime that is usually spent reading or making phone calls. Why not strike up a conversation with another business-looking person? Ask them how often they travel for work and what the nature of their business is.

This same principle applies when you are sitting in the lounge of the service area of the local car dealer or standing in line at the coffee shop. There really isn't a venue where it is impossible to engage someone in a conversation.

I have always treated the staff of my clients with the utmost kindness and respect. These staffers have private lives that can also be a source for your business. Maybe they are volunteer firemen or involved with their local church or civic organization. All of these are more opportunities to expand your network.

So here is just one more example of how it always pays to be NICE, which stands for "Nobody Is Considered Excused" – from your pool of potential clients, that is. Always go if invited, especially if it costs you money. Doing this weeds out all of the people who are just looking for a free lunch and puts you in contact with those who are as serious about meeting people as you are.

Always wear a company name tag, or at least the sticker one that is provided at the door. Write your name clearly, and if you have terrible handwriting like me, ask the nice person sitting at the sign-in desk to write it for you. It defeats the purpose of paying for a nice event to go around wearing something no one can read. Wear it on the right side of your chest because that is where the eye travels to first.

In summary, think of pretty much every area of your life as an opportunity to network. You never know who you will meet and where you will meet the person that could help you with a career-changing partnership. Be kind, be nice, and be patient, and you'll win the networking game in the end.

Howie Mann has worked at Pitney Bowes, a Fortune 500 firm and became their youngest sales manager at 23 years old.

He went on to become the national sales director for a silver firm that supplied the Vatican with flatware. Later, he started his my own copier firm and became a leading Canon dealer from 1996 to 2016. After selling this firm, he became a money lender to businesses and real estate investors. It is now Howie's pleasure to help businesses and investors fulfill their dreams with the initial capital that they need. He works with banking and private lending partners to make this happen for them. It has been his true pleasure to work on projects such as homeless shelters, softball stadiums, restaurants, apartment and office buildings, and so much more.

The Work of an Olympian
Scott Mason

I.The Work of Olympians

A pebble thrown into water changes a pond. A chance meeting can change a life. An entrepreneur's vision can change the world. Changing the world is no task for a mortal. It's the task of something greater. It's the task of a god.

And that is a statement not made lightly. Think about it. The entrepreneur does not simply have an idea, then let it waft away into the ether. She doesn't just take the next step and will it into reality -- which is itself a profound act of creation. She nurtures that idea. She sets it up to grow and flourish. She populates it with people. And, like a god, she has the power to destroy it .... and everything within.

To truly live this entrepreneurial life -- to embody everything that entrepreneurialism is and can be -- is to assume and accept an awesome power, and an indescribable responsibility. To succeed requires power and perseverance that are beyond the reach of all but most rarified of beings. If this business is sustainable, it can even lead to a kind of immortality.

This is why the greatest entrepreneurs in history have achieved almost mythical status. And why we all have a responsibility to understand and appreciate the role of entrepreneurialism, and our roles as entrepreneurs, in the epic mythology that defines the human experience. In that meta-mythology, our role is singular. It is Olympian.

On even the most superficial reflection, that fact is obvious. Think about Zeus, the chief of the ancient Greek gods. He was born into a world ruled by the Titans, giant primeval beings whose work had created a previously unheard-of era of prosperity and glory. But the Titans were not particularly flexible or capable of change. In fact, even after receiving a warning that a new generation of gods could overthrow them, their leader, Cronus, chose not to adapt. Instead, Cronus chose to cannibalize his own children, much as older, larger businesses literally eat threatening upstarts.

But one of those upstarts, Zeus, outsmarted Cronus. Perhaps it was inevitable. The Roman version of Cronus, named Saturn, represented time -- as in time passing by. In any event, Zeus didn't want to live in Cronus' world; he wanted to build his own palace and shape the world in a newer, more dynamic way. He was, perhaps, the world's first entrepreneur.

Like the best start-up owners, Zeus figured out a way to outsmart Cronus; eventually, with a lot of work, he overthrew the Titans. Zeus then went about building his own magnificent citadel on Mount Olympus. Because he couldn't do everything himself, Zeus gave specific domain responsibilities and delegated executive management of his empire to other deities. Some sat in the central Olympian headquarters; others worked in field offices, such as the sea. Most were gods that had had direct ties to Zeus, but he also gave major roles to a few representatives of the old order who had proven amenable to change. More specific task responsibilities were given to various spirits, minor gods, and sprites who became staff. All of them believed in Zeus' mission and worked to create a new world. Zeus, of course, rewarded them generously. And an enterprise that we all discuss thousands of years later was born.

An interesting aspect of Greek mythology is that, within the myths, the actions of the lead characters exist in order to demonstrate that they are worthy of being mythologized. In other words, many of the myths seem to assume that the characters know that they can create a mythical framework. And therein lies an important point: *we have the power to create our own mythology.* We can change the mythology of the past. And mythology is the architecture of our future.

The implications are profound. Knowing that you have the power to create your own mythology allows you to dislodge toxic myths that might keep Olympus from expressing its full grandeur in the world. It allows you to ignite the same charisma that has kept us talking about the Olympic gods for millennia. It allows you a type of freedom that is unimaginable to others. It might -- just might -- give you a taste of immortality.

Is that something you want?

If so, read on. We'll talk about how to make it happen.

II. One Man's Myths

The most famous analysis of myth as a framework for modern living was made through the work of legendary literature professor and author Joseph Campbell. Campbell is best known for detailed analysis of the so-called "monomyth," or hero's journey, that he claimed dominated mythical storytelling across cultures. While his work has had a tremendous impact in popular culture, suffice it to say that his conclusions are controversial.

Outside of the heroic myths, those who study folklore and mythology have identified various other myth types that you, as an entrepreneur, may actually find more meaningful. While no "canon" of myth types actually exists, here are some that you may find relevant:

- *Origin* – stories of the past; what made us who we are.
- *Apocalyptic* – predictions of doom in the future
- *Social* – justifications for living life based on pre-existing social rules or expectations
- *Ritual* – explanations for self-sabotaging behavior patterns
- *Chthonic* – related to the underworld; tales of living in spiritual or emotional darkness

During my many years working anonymously in faceless and decidedly Titan-like large organizations, the myths I told myself and others had every one of these elements, packed in a mental space that was smaller (and more tightly-screwed) than Pandora's Box. And, as you can imagine, the saga was not a pretty one. Here it is: judge for yourself.

The origin myth: I was born in glitzy, diverse, and sophisticated London, England. But my parents, a white British woman and a law student from Trinidad, did not want me. They put me up for adoption as an infant; I was adopted by a working-class couple from the United States who raised me in a rural area of Kansas. My adoptive parents were African-American in an overwhelmingly white and conservative community without opportunity and where racial and other prejudices were open and frequently shameless. In short, I had been abandoned and banished to a part of the world where I was destined to be miserable.

The apocalyptic myth: My debate coach once told the entire class about me: "You can teach a monkey how to speak, but you can't teach it to think." He was right. I got into a good law school and college, but, ironically, it was only because of my limited intellect. I had to work hard and with tremendous discipline to compensate, and eventually that, along with luck, got me into a good college and, later, through law school. I worked even harder and with more ambition to get ahead in large organizational life, but that was just because, without the financial success, titles, and great office, everyone's belief about my limitations would be proven true, and the shame of exposure would be unbearable. But, as coffee grounds always sink to the bottom, I always knew that the horrible truth would emerge. I just wanted to see some sun before falling back into the cellar.

The social myth: I always talked back to my parents and so that meant I should be a lawyer. In any event, law was guaranteed to give me access to power and money. Plus, no one would ever call an attorney stupid. In order to have the social prestige someone like me needed to succeed, I *had* to become an attorney.

The ritual myth: In order to get ahead, and be anything in life, I needed to look and act a certain way. That included speaking in a way that exuded authority, but not vulnerability, and being cautious about expressing emotions that were not positive unless the emotion was anger. I needed to stomp on my colleagues or else they would stomp on me. And I needed to wear a blue or gray suit with a tie and a white or light blue shirt at all times.

The chthonic myth: Happiness or joy on the job was for other people, not me. Spirituality and meaning at work were unprofessional and, frankly, only for the weak or naive. No one truly cared about me; I could not afford to truly care for others. Any generosity shown to me was just a ploy for power, exploitation of my skills, or a promotion. I would work, retire, then die. That was that.

You might not be surprised to learn that if there was any mythological figure I could have seen myself in, it was Hades, Lord of the Underworld. Feared and despised by the other gods, Hades was cast out of Olympus and had to make his home literally beneath the earth. Although his underground domain was home to most of the world's wealth (after all, most minerals come from mines), Hades did not enjoy it. It brought him no pleasure at all. And even with the power and magnificence of the other gods, his demeanor was grim and his heart pitiless. When he wanted something, he took it -- most notably, his luckless wife, Persephone, whom he kidnapped and kept imprisoned for half of every year. He had no hope, either. His fate was to stay in the underworld forever.

He – and I – did not live the life of an Olympian.

Where did it take me? Well, I did, in a sense, succeed. I ended up in C-level positions of two major organizations and had leadership roles in projects that should have made any professional proud. But my heart was clogged. My health suffered: I developed high blood pressure, rosacea in the face, and a seemingly endless round of physical ailments and injuries. When I presented to the world, I came off as boring, bureaucratic, evasive, and angry. And I felt trapped. I couldn't even imagine a different life. In fact, when people told me they loved their jobs, I either laughed in disbelief or slack-jawedly stared, as if they had said words in another language. That's because I was so far gone that I couldn't even comprehend the idea of someone being happy with their professional life. They might as well have been an antelope, bursting with joy while being ripped to pieces and eaten alive by a crocodile.

III. Journey to Freedom

Eventually, the day came when I had to live or die by my myths. After nearly twenty years working as an attorney and senior executive at massive governmental agencies, a badly deteriorating relationship with my final agency head led us to mutually agree to my departure. Although I left on my own terms, the circumstances were far less than ideal and it was during a time of nearly record unemployment throughout the United States – especially for seasoned former executives whose salary demands were, employers assumed, going to be high.

Despite having an Ivy League law degree, a genuinely impressive resume, and demonstrable leadership skills, after more than a year had passed with endless job applications that went nowhere, I hit a breaking point. My savings were getting terrifyingly low, my employment prospects were close to zero with no signs of improvement, and my previous cold indifference to hope was beginning to turn into outright despair. The iron statue of Hades that best captured who I was had feet made of clay, and they were crumbling. And when I finally toppled, I could not imagine how I would ever rise up again.

It's hard to describe the extent of my hopelessness. There were nights when I couldn't sleep, sometimes because I was overwhelmed with fear, sometimes because of existential rage at the universe, and sometimes because of extraordinary shame and grief. Honestly, there were days when had it not been for the heart and ears of my spouse, I'm not sure I would have survived.

Luckily, eventually, a friend of mine introduced me to a very well-known martial artist who was looking for some strategic legal help to support the growth of the dojos he owned. This man had, like me, come from humble roots but, unlike me, had created his own, unique Olympus, and was imagining a future that was, in its own way, as visionary as Zeus'. He truly believed in the power of entrepreneurialism and how it could change the world. Before we met, I had walked among and known hundreds of entrepreneurs and small business owners, but never truly "seen" them. However, my friend was someone whose passion and vision could not be ignored.

He believed I would make a good entrepreneur. I observed his life and wanted something like that for myself. He also challenged me to become a martial artist. One minor myth I'd held was that activities like Brazilian Jiu-Jitsu were just not "me." But his persistence in calling that out fable as the mental invention it was, with no basis in truth, eventually led me to start taking classes at his schools. I became a martial artist – and, for the first time, totally dislodged a bit of my own toxic personal mythology.

"How many other myths about myself were untrue?" I began to wonder. Maybe that I had to be an attorney and an executive wearing a suit in order to be somebody in this world was a false myth. And, with that idea planted in my head, although it took years to get there, eventually the seeds took root; my reinvention as an entrepreneur began.

Since then, I've learned to question all of those myths that held me back and kept me living a life that was horrible and Hadean. I realized that just as, somewhere along the line, I had either accepted them, based on the words of others, or simply made them up, I had the power to reframe them. Rather than seeing the challenges that triggered my toxic mythmaking as Herculean hurdles, I came to see them as the authors of my purpose – as psychic chains that I'd manacled around myself but could unshackle.

As I absorbed that, I began the difficult, but intensely rewarding, process of rewriting my mythology – creating a blueprint for a unique and truly singular set of palaces built to my exact specifications. I did that by undergoing an extensive internal archaeological dig to uncover my strengths and connect them to inner truths and values that were waiting for a chance to be self-expressed. And how my myths reshaped themselves were epic.

The *origin myth* of a boy abandoned at birth, raised unwanted in the dusty hinterlands, became the myth of a child whose journey across the ocean represented a psychological rebirth – a rebirth that taught him how to reinvent himself again when the need for change arose. The *doomsday myth* which inevitably ended in my professional destruction developed a new coda, marked by something even more profound: professional resurrection, just like the famous Heracles did after his body burned to ash. The *social myth* necessitating my career as an attorney became one where my unique personality could be translated into singular star-power. The *ritual myth*, which put me in boring suits, boring people to death with legalese? It was replaced by a willingness to ignite the inner charisma that came with recreating a whole new mythology about who I am and what is possible for me. And that charisma was – and still is – buoyed by the inner radiance that emerged once I learned that the release of my uniqueness could be expressed in the world through entrepreneurialism – a radiance that took me right out of the underworld of *chthonic myth* and to the top of the sky-dome.

In a sense, igniting the charisma that suddenly emerged once I had completed the internal archaeological dig and rewritten the myths was the key to making the most of the professional freedom that joy-centered entrepreneurialism can bring. "Charisma" is more than just a big stage presence or dramatic gesticulations. In fact, a dramatic personality or high energy level isn't necessarily a part of charisma at all.

The word "charisma" itself comes from Greek mythology. It was named after the goddess Charis. She was also known as "Aglaea," which literally means *splendor* or *brilliance*. To the Greeks, charisma was marked by charm, human creativity, and abundance. It was also associated with the concept of brightness. Their definition holds up. Toxic myths poison your soul and imprison it in a psychological netherworld. But you release yourself from them and write new ones for your future, charm – love of and selfless engagement with others – and explosive creativity clean out the inner valves that were clogging up your heart. The brilliance of your charming and creative self-expression attracts others to you … and when others are attracted to you, abundance follows. In other words, your charisma – your freedom to be you – acts like an opportunity magnet. With charisma and opportunity, bolstered on an understanding of those inner strengths unearthed during your archaeological expedition, financial freedom is all but inevitable.

IV. Other Myths

The toxic myths I carried around are by no means the only ones, or universal. Although large groups of myths tend to fall into broad categories, the substance of individuals' myths can be as varied as humanity itself. That being said, there are some common toxic fables that entrepreneurs tell themselves, that you may recognize in yourself or others. Here are three, along with their more accurate counterparts.

• ***Intelligence, a good idea, and hard work alone will make you a success in business.*** While this one has a superficial appeal, and no one would argue that intelligence and hard work help or that a good idea isn't absolutely essential, it also ignores the reality that entrepreneurialism is also a game of wits (including humor). We all want to be Zeus, but don't forget we all need a little Hermes inside us, too.

Hermes was the god of those who live by their wits -- including small businesspeople ("merchants") and comics. He, like the primal supporters of Zeus, was an innovator and an inventor (the lyre), knew how to be scrappy (he put brooms on the tails of some cows he stole in order to cover their tracks), had a whole cape full of magic tricks just in case of an emergency, was ludicrously glib (investors would have loved him), and even got away with causing the death of a 100-eyed giant by making his judges laugh. Make sure that your mythical repertoire includes a lot of Hermes.

. . .

• ***You're not allowed to be afraid or overwhelmed.*** When his grandmother sent the heinous monsters Echidna and Typhon to destroy Zeus and his burgeoning dynasty, Zeus was so scared that he fled to Egypt and turned into an animal. However, his daughter Athena -- the goddess of wisdom -- called him out on his fear: she held him accountable. He regained his courage and managed to defeat Typhon. If Zeus can be afraid, so can you. Just be sure to have someone wise around to hold YOU accountable. It's an important way of keeping all of your own apocalyptic myths at bay.

• ***A successful entrepreneur doesn't need a mentor or a coach.*** Even Zeus needed a mentor, to help him both overthrow Cronus and build the new world afterward. His mentor was named Metis, the goddess of Prudence. Their child ended up being the above-mentioned Athena, the goddess of wisdom and strategy. Athena literally burst out of Zeus' brain – and she also ended up counseling her father, too. This represented the idea that a great leader needs both advice on the practical and tactical (Metis) and the long-term, big-picture (Athena).

That these coaches were both women in a patriarchal culture is not insignificant. Zeus' acceptance of mentoring from women represented a sublimation of his ego in exchange for the gift of knowledge. The ego-based myth that you don't need a mentor or coach is perhaps the most toxic of the chthonic, or "underworld," myths – and it can literally keep you in an entrepreneurial Hades forever. Zeus learned a new myth; others can learn from his example.

V. A New Avatar

For years, while walking the large, forbidding hallways of large offices or enduring the false cheer of workplaces whose splashes of color hid crushing blights of the soul, when I would look in the mirror, I would see a version of Hades – a hard, stony exterior barely containing a volcano of anger and suffering wrapped around a soulless black hole within. I had no soul. I had no charisma. I had no freedom. I was a walking human void.

Today, with my toxic myths banished forever, I have all of those things, and so much more. My new avatar is Helios, the glorious god of the Sun. In Greek myths, the eternally vibrant Helios has not one, but two massive palaces: one on the eastern edge of the world, the other on the west. Strong and vibrant, every day, he takes a golden chariot and rides it to the summit of the sky, where he sees all. Helios thus is the guardian of oaths – the personification of truthfulness. His inner brilliance – his charisma – ignites again and again, every morning, and shines so brightly that a mortal literally cannot bear to look at it. It is bright enough to light the entire world. That light nourishes, feeds, and brings animation to everything it touches. And only Helios can command the chariot's horses, whose path runs through the sky-spanning zodiac. Not even Zeus would dare to handle them or interfere with his work. Helios is thus truly free. And the gold of his chariot and stallions represents the abundance that he both brings and is cloaked in.

Helios is a far cry from Hades. In fact, it might be the most extreme avatar switcheroo possible. But that simply shows how far a conscious effort to release and replace toxic myths can take a committed entrepreneur. Dislodge your own toxic myths. Ignite your inner charisma. Magnetize and monetize your professional freedom. Make this entrepreneurial life Olympic.

Scott Mason is a speaker, author, podcaster, and coach who works with executives and successful entrepreneurs feeling stuck or stagnant in their career or business — and are ready for a change. After graduating from Columbia Law School, Scott worked for over 20 years as an attorney and senior executive with a variety of organizations in the government and the nonprofit sectors before successfully growing and scaling a manufacturing company. His insights on leadership and transformation have appeared in both book compilations and online magazines such as *Authority*, *Medium*, and *CEO*

Blog Nation; the listenership of his podcast, *Scott Mason's Purpose Highway,* is in the top 5% globally. He combines his wealth of large organizational and entrepreneurial experience with a long-lasting and deep love of Greek mythology – with all of its fun, excitement and deeper, universal meanings – to help his clients dislodge their toxic myths to ignite charisma within, and then magnetize and monetize professional freedom.

Fall Off the Grid and You Run the Risk of Losing the Business and the Contact

By Adrian Miller

W hy do so many sales professionals build great relationships with prospects, networking contacts, and referral sources only to allow themselves to fall off the grid and join the ranks of those that are out of sight and out of mind? Indeed, it's a very sad place to find yourself.

Many years ago, I found myself falling off of the prospect's radar screen never to get my "return on time" (ROT) that I had expended on this individual. We had met for lunch, talked business and did the discovery dance, and I was confident that there would soon be a project that we would work on together.

I followed up once and then a second time, and decided to "age" the name, leaving him to lie dormant for about 8 weeks. I thought that was the perfect amount of time to reconnect.

I thought wrong! A competitor had made their way to his doorstep a month after our lunch. They worked their magic and secured the business opportunity before I could circle back.

You could say that I "educated" the prospect and laid the groundwork for the competitor making it easier for them to win the business because the prospect was more "primed" to buy.

Or you could point out that I allowed myself to be forgotten by not showing value and building the relationship BEFORE there was a "real" business relationship. The truth is that is exactly what happened, and I vowed to never let it happen again.

The common – and wrong – conclusion focuses on the prospect, networking contact or referral source - they aren't ready, they don't have a connection for you, there is no introduction for them to make, and so on. The right answer – the one that you can do something about – doesn't focus on the other individual, it focuses on you. In other words, this is about **maintaining mindshare**.

Mindshare is the amount of attention you garner when in the middle of a long sales or networking cycle, and as such, don't easily "have" the face, ear, or eye of your prospect or contact. Mindshare is the **art** of staying on the radar screen without becoming a pain in the butt.

To begin, you must shy away "checking in" or "touching base."

The fundamental truth is that you must add value to the relationship every step of the way and do so right from the beginning. By doing anything less, your prospects and contacts will either forget about you or lean back in dismay every time they receive your email or call.

So how do you accomplish this? Easy, use the three I's:

Introductions

Our contacts are our lifeblood and include existing clients, dormant accounts, networking resources, business contacts, and people that received your proposal but decided to not work with you.

Connect them!

Introduce two people for the following reasons:

- They work with the same types of clients but do different things
- Their businesses are very synergistic, and they can potentially collaborate on opportunities
- They are equally passionate about a hobby
- They can use each other's services

Be proactive when making your introductions. Waiting for someone to ask you "do you know ...." is not the way to effectively "stay on the grid," and the opportunities to be a "connector" will be far and few between.

I'm an *introduction zealot*. I'm especially excited when I put people together and their relationship flourishes far beyond my wildest expectations, where the business is ongoing and keeps expanding past the original business opportunity. It doesn't always happen that way, but when it does, it's like a gift that keeps on giving.

I've had the good fortune to make many of these introductions including one that turned into tens of thousands of dollars in revenue. And to think, it all started with "I'd like to introduce you to _____. I think that you two can network well together."

If you are interested in staying on the grid and adding bottom-line value, making introductions is the way to go.

Invitations

Business conferences, webinars, networking gatherings, and Association events fill the time slots on our calendar, and while it is impossible to attend everything, many events will shoot up to the top of your "must attend" list. The others are quickly deleted and soon forgotten because you don't think there is any value or you've run out of available time

But just because you don't have the time to attend doesn't mean that you can't share the invitation with your contacts. It's actually a win-win-win for all:

- The event manager or group leader is happy to get additional attendees
- The person with whom you share the invite will be happy to learn about new events and meetings
- You become front and center not because you are "checking in" but because you have shared something of value

Sharing invitations is easy. They show up in your email every day and all you need to do is remember to forward the email before you hit delete!

Information

Thanks to the Internet, sharing valuable information is just a keystroke away. Stay close and add recognizable value by sending links to Ted Talks, webinars, articles and white papers. The shared information does not always have to be relevant to the recipient's specific business and can also focus on hobbies or other interests they may have.

For instance, I greatly appreciate receiving information about travel so anyone that sends me a link to an article or video gets my immediate attention. It may seem silly, but they have captured my interest because they have clearly given some thought to what would interest ME.

Sharing information takes a bit more time than forwarding links to events and is not as highly personal as an introduction but helps to position you as a thought leader and someone with diverse interests.

The 3 I's takes care of the "what" you can do; but, as you know, in sales "how" is just as important; if not more so:

- Focus on your contact and don't be self-serving in your touch points. It has to be interesting to THEM.
- Avoid any sense of entitlement -- simply because you've met them face to face and had a good lunch

meeting or whatever doesn't mean that you're owed a referral or business.

- Never do the "I haven't heard from you in for a little/long while and I'm just calling to touch base" thing. It implies that your contact dropped the ball – and this is often not the case. They aren't your client yet, and there's no agreement in place that outlines their role, if any, in working together. Until they convert from prospect to client, there's no ball for them to drop or pick up.
- Remember that your prospective client and networking contacts are probably in contact with many other business resources and therefore they have options. Allowing yourself to be forgotten means that they will research these options and you may no longer be "in the picture."

In business, many speak of ROI (return on investment), however, I prefer to take into account ROT (return on time), specifically the time it took to:

- Research the company or individual
- Initiate the relationship
- Grow the relationship

If you let yourself become invisible or give up on them too soon you will not have the opportunity to get your ROT, and if you do that often enough, over time that is a recipe for losing money.

In no particular order, Adrian Miller is a sales consultant, trainer, author, avid traveler, amateur photographer, theater lover, movie goer and networker extraordinaire.

She launched her sales consulting business 3 decades ago and since then has worked in pretty much every industry and with companies large and small. She brings passion and enthusiasm to every engagement and is well known for her sense of humor and highly practical and results-driven approach that she takes with all of her clients.

Adrian is the author of "The Blatant Truth: 50 Ways to Sales Success," "The Blatant Truth: How to Not Screw Up The Customer Service Game," and "Dispatches From the Frontline: Musings on Sales, Business Development and Networking" a collection of her popular articles and blog posts.

Looking for a new place to network, Adrian also created Adrian's Network, an incredibly innovative and immensely successful business networking community that has raised the bar for anyone that is interested in connecting, collaborating and community.

Eight Lies Business Leaders Tell Themselves
By Jeri Quinn

A re you a business leader? Whether you own your own business or you're a department leader inside a bigger company, you look at yourself in the mirror each day and say, am I doing a good job? Am I developing my potential, growing my business, helping my staff be more productive, doing the right things and doing them the right way? Is this work fulfilling me? Am I happy?

You're to be congratulated if those questions get you curious enough to read about the eight lies below. Why build your business (and your role in it) on a house of cards?

Here are some lies that my coaching clients deal with. They eventually get to realize these assumptions are lies and then wonder what took them so long, since they could have been realizing benefits all along the way. I present these lies business leaders tell themselves to you to see if any resonate. If even one does, it's a wakeup call. Take some action. It will make all the difference.

1. **"I don't have any blind spots. Okay, I'll say I have a few just so people will feel that I'm human. But really I don't know what they could possibly be. So I won't search out any blind spots. I certainly won't go on a fishing expedition with a coach or mentor to help me find any. That's a waste of time and money."**

Are you sure that you're not afraid you might find some blind spots? And that might necessitate you having to change something? Ohh! That bad word "change." It might be a change in mindset, a change in perspective, some uncertainty. And Heaven forbid – a change in behavior! You might have to communicate with others differently or do something out of your comfort zone. You might have to shake some complacency and ask some tough questions.

There are assessments so you can ascertain your strengths and your blind spots. One decision making assessment especially points out if you prefer making decisions based on emotional impact on people or practical ramifications or whether or not the action fits a system. You have a favorite, so does everyone. When you find your favorite, you'll also find your blind spot. Then you can do something about it to make more well-rounded decisions.

You might seek out input from someone who doesn't have that blind spot. Then your business will be more productive, more responsive to the market, more sensitive to employee concerns or be able to do things your blind spots just wouldn't allow before.

2. "Working really hard gets me ahead. The harder I work, the more I get done, the more results I see. Well, maybe, I hope to see. I'm planting seeds, more and more seeds. Something will sprout sooner or later. I'm an entrepreneur and all entrepreneurs work hard."

Many of our western civilization parents embraced the culture of working hard incessantly. We know the slogan "work smarter, not harder." Yet, even though we want to be strategic, we get sucked into the addictive lifestyle of working, working, working, often without boundaries. This makes us feel important. We feel like we're following in parental footsteps. Yet, have you asked your spouse and kids how it impacts them? And don't take an excuse or muttering under their breath as a real answer. Ask them to be frank because you want to know. When you work all the time, do they miss your engagement in their lives? How does it impact all the things they were hoping to do together?

Now think about those people who have created businesses where they delegate? They have fun every day. They're not locked into a work, work, work schedule. They travel, take Fridays off, spend weekends that are restful or adventurous, get more accomplished through others than they could ever do themselves. It takes creating boundaries to protect your time. It takes hiring the right person and training them till you can trust them to work independently, then delegating without micromanaging. A little difficult for a workaholic, but very rewarding. Just think of it this way, after your first heart attack, you'll be forced to slow down. So why not do it now? Put more fun in your life and avoid the heart attack.

3. "Nobody can do it better than me. I started this company. I developed the service and the winning formula for customer support. Nobody can implement it like I can. Nobody can talk to the client like I can. Nobody can negotiate with our vendors and distributors like I can. I try to train other people to do it just like I do it. But they never seem to get it right. I might as well do it myself."

This is what keeps your company small. You only have 24 hours in a day. You can't possibly do every full- time job yourself. You can't even do multiple part-time jobs well, because you don't have specialized skills in all those areas. Besides, are your training skills so poor that you can't trust that you could train someone to get better and better? Don't you feel you deserve better?

Is there only one way to do things? If you allowed someone else to bring their creativity and ingenuity into a situation, maybe they'd find a better way. What comes to mind is a story about a company that had a big problem, something they recently discovered that was going to be a big critical issue if they didn't get it solved right away. So all the right minds were called into a meeting to brainstorm the answer to this problem. They talked and talked. But no one had an answer. As they left the meeting, they noted the young guy, the new employee, hadn't even seemed to want to help. He pretty much was just playing with his phone. About an hour later the young guy walks into the project manager's office and said, "I've got it. This is how you solve the problem. I checked with my friends and one of them just had the same problem."

There are many ways to solve problems. If you never allow people the autonomy to do things in new ways, all the good employees will leave, the ones who are left will never try, and your business will suffer.

4. "I listen to feedback so I'm OK in that department. I acknowledge people's opinions and that's enough. I've read business books that tell me to acknowledge everyone's input. So I do. Then I do what I think is best."

Have you really listened to other's input? Or did you just hear them to check off the listening "box" without really considering their input?

Very often business leaders are impervious to the comments of others. In the back of their minds they're thinking, "Yes, others need to make their comments publicly and they need to be thanked. That's a show so they can be placated. But the comments don't really have to matter. I've earned the right to make my decisions. You don't know what I know. You haven't seen what I've seen. So I'm putting up a shield. My role gives me legitimacy. So I don't have to really consider that feedback or input. It's basically all about me and what I think is best. Plus, if I say it loud enough and with enough personal power, it will come across as good leadership and executive presence."

The alternative is humble leadership, servant leadership, where you don't place the focus on yourself, you place the focus on the organization. Jim Collins in his book *Good to Great* describes Level 5 Leaders, the ones who generated the highest levels of success, as self-effacing, quiet, reserved, and sometimes shy. They motivated the enterprise more with inspired standards than with an inspiring personality. They welcomed feedback, co-created with others who were at lower levels and closer to the actual work. They let others create options and guided their thinking to include things beyond their purview and then arrived at decisions together. This allows the teams to have buy-in into the work to be implemented. Better productivity, engagement, and morale ensue. The co-creation model of leadership is much more effective and not possible if you're buying into the lie that you as the leader make decisions best because of your experience or role.

5. "If my people were unhappy, they'd tell me. I'm a good boss. I'm approachable. I have an open-door policy. I listen to feedback. If there were something wrong, somebody would tell me."

No, they probably won't tell you. They probably don't feel you want to know. Did you ever ask? They might tell you about something that matters to them. Racheal walks into your open door and tells you about a problem with HR. Your two direct reports can't work out a solution, so they come in to ask your advice and really just want to complain about each other, hoping you'll side with one of them.

But do they come in and say the culture stinks? That they don't know the vision of the company? That they wouldn't recommend a friend or family member to work there? That they have a hard time getting out of bed in the morning to come to another dreary day at work? That they need inspiration? Do they ever ask for appreciation?

You have to proactively ask those questions. Have you done a culture survey? Do you take direct reports out to lunch occasionally, and ask how you can be a better boss or company leader? Do you really listen to their suggestions, make changes and then get back to them and ask, "How am I doing?"

Do you have company meetings where you define the company's vision and values? When you talk about what's coming up next and why? Do you bring in clients to talk about how the work your employees have done has made an impact? Do you praise and appreciate your employees publicly, so they feel really good about themselves and the role they play in your company?

It's not enough to lead by sitting behind your desk and hoping your employees will reach out to you to form a trusting relationship. You as the business leader are in a position of authority and can be a little intimidating, even though you don't intend to be. You have to proactively reach out, be welcoming, stimulate the relationships, know your people personally, proactively give them a good experience in your meetings, and establish trust. You get to give them information/inspiration so they can ask questions about vision, values, company direction, some personal info, some stories, empathy. Showing each employee that you care about them individually and that you'll go more than halfway to create a relationship will make all the difference in your retention rate, your suggestions box, the team's productivity, and your bottom line.

6. "I don't have to do strategic planning. I don't have to be proactive and go after big goals. I can go along with the flow and do business as usual."

When my clients say this, I hear the complacency in their voices. "Things are working all right so far, so why rock the boat? We're providing something everyone wants. Sales are pretty good. All we have to do is keep it up. That's hard enough."

The problem is that the world keeps moving forward. Wayne Gretsky, hockey star, says, "I skate to where the puck is going to be." If you're not continually making improvements, your industry is ripe for disruption. Look at the taxi industry and Uber/Lyft. Look at the hotel industry and Airbnb. It won't be long before some young company figures out a way to beat you at your own game, doing it cheaper, faster, and giving a better user experience.

Crisis is another word for opportunity. In the great depression and the 2008-2009 recession, many new companies were born. More companies had R&D going on during these times and the innovators were the ones who captured the most market share coming out of each downturn.

Another quote I regularly use with my clients is, "When the wind blows, some people build walls, and some people build windmills." Certainly, we've had our share of pandemic-related obstacles recently. If anything, it's created change and "the next normal." If you want your business to be relevant in a changing world, you have to adapt.

Strategic planning is all about assessing those changes in the "next normal," figuring out how they apply to your industry, and creating a plan to adapt to stay relevant. It requires the contributions of many stakeholders, certainly senior staff, possibly clients and vendors, maybe market researchers or other advisors. Research is done to report on trends in your industry and your clients' industries. What will they need, and can we proactively be getting ready? Will our chain of distribution or vendor supply chain be disrupted? How can we get ahead of that curve? How can we prevent threats to our business? How can we take advantage of opportunities emerging in a changing world? What does the budget look like for what we want to do? Does our staffing need to change? Our technology?

The strategic planning process can be a big overhaul or a minimal updating if you did a deep dive last year. The companies that don't do this may be in for a rude awakening and the leader who is buying into the lie that it's not necessary may not be a leader for long.

7. "I'm flexible. I go with what the market demands. I'm like the tree that bends in the wind. It's okay to change my tune to be responsive to the needs of clients and employees. I have to go with what works. I'm a survivor."

This makes you a follower, not a leader. What do you stand for? Great leaders earn the trust of their followers by having a spine, not by changing every time the wind blows a different way. Great leaders stand for integrity and truth telling, even when it hurts. They stand for fairness and respect, even when it's not popular. They lead with values that guide behavior and they set those values up as conditions for employment in their organizations. When the organization is based on decency, empowerment, fairness, and integrity, the workplace becomes safe and employees become more productive. They spend less time looking over their shoulders to see what threat is coming next, and they spend more time being productive and collaborative. Yes, flexibility can be a good thing, but not when it comes to behaving out of alignment with core values.

Often, we say or do things unconsciously that are not in alignment with the values we espouse. Who in your life challenges you and gets you to examine a behavior? Who asks the tough question: Does what you just say/do, or what you're planning to say/do, align with the person you want to be, a person who lives by the guidelines you've defined? Your confidence and your inner strength will come from you standing up for what's right. It will ripple out all around you and become your legacy. You'll be a role model for others in your workplace (as well as for your kids at home).

8. "We're just having a run of bad luck. It's the economy, it's the pandemic. Everyone in my industry is down. Our bank won't lend us the money. Our customers can't/won't pay us. Our biggest client had a change in ownership, and they went with the new owner's vendor."

The common thread through each of these statements is the status of victimhood. Everyone else is at fault and is doing something bad to us. You're seeing the glass half empty.

What if you were to reframe and see these obstacles as opportunities to grow, discover new more relevant ways to address a changing work ecosystem? It really is a mindset shift to seeing the glass half full.

My mom always told me, "You get what you tolerate." If your standards are low and you expect a low level of compliance, business, profits, work, anything, that's what you 'll get. But if you organically expect a higher level of those things, you'll do what it takes to meet your expectations.

I think that's what it means when you hear gurus state, "You can create anything you want." What they are saying is that if you want a higher level of success, and really believe that you deserve it, and your expectation is that nothing at a lower level is even being considered, then you will achieve what you want because you won't tolerate the lower level. It's not part of your identity.

Victimhood is a lie because we all have choice.

Your Choice!

What kind of leader do you want to be? You've now read through eight lies that you might be telling yourself. They may not all apply to you. But the ones that do…? You've been given fair warning, and the bell can't be unrung. You can stick your head in the sand and pretend you never read them, or that they don't apply to you. But then you have to look in the mirror every morning and ask those questions:

Am I doing a good job?

Am I developing my potential, growing my business, helping my staff be more productive, doing the right things and doing them the right way?

Is this work fulfilling me?

Am I happy?

Will you create more lies or will you be honest with yourself? Your future depends on it.

Jeri Quinn is the founder and president of Driving Improved Results, a professional training and development firm. She's a serial entrepreneur having built, run and sold a technology firm, a human services consultancy, and a marketing firm. Her current company helps organizations achieve goals, reduce turnover, save money, exceed customer expectations and attract talent. She and her team of experienced professionals coach, consult, facilitate and instruct in leadership, communication, project management, lean six sigma, presentation skills, customer service, job benchmarking and candidate selection. She's especially proud of their accomplishments in building high performing teams, training managers to manage, and coaching executives to make tough decisions in uncertain times. She's also an author of two business books about Customer Loyalty and Business Partnering. The purpose of her life is to empower others and she's done that as a parent, teacher, a therapist, an employer and now as an executive/business coach. While business is fun and exciting, it can always be enhanced by sharing some dark chocolate, a glass of prosecco and lots of dancing. www.DrivingImprovedResults.com

How to Get More Business from the People You Know
By Edie Reinhardt

Have you ever experienced the snowball effect of referrals?

One of my clients got a referral from BA someone he met years earlier when they were both doing work for a business owner as outside consultants. The referred client (RF) ended up hiring my client, but it didn't end there. RF also needed other help outside my client's area of expertise so my client recommended one of his long-standing contacts (CC) who was then hired. Shortly thereafter, CC asked my client to join in on a pitch to another prospect and they were both hired for that.

While some of this might have happened without any extra effort on my client's part, the reality is that he consistently markets to existing contacts to increase the likelihood they will remember him when an opportunity comes along.

Generating additional revenue from existing clients and contacts is usually easier and more cost-effective than trying to bring in wholly new leads. Yet many businesses don't pay enough attention to this side of marketing and business development. The people you know can become first time or repeat clients, refer prospects to you, or introduce you to good referral sources. That doesn't mean you should neglect trying to expand your reach and attract other leads. Your marketing plan should detail strategies for promoting your business to both current and new people. However, this article focuses on how to leverage existing contacts with five steps to get your started.

Review and prioritize your contacts

Many business experts recommend putting your existing clients into 3 buckets – A, B, and C – based on how valuable they are or could be to you. The same rule should apply to past clients, referral sources, friends, colleagues and others you know. Develop a plan and allocate resources to each group as follows:

• Bucket A has the most valuable people. They represent past and current clients and referrals sources who think highly of your work, you have a good relationship with them and they would give you a glowing reference if asked. They may also have connections that could benefit you. You want to give A people the most personal attention and think about how you can maintain a strong relationship. Make sure you stay in touch with them regularly and don't be afraid to ask them for assistance. However, consistently offer them value before asking for their help.

• • •

• Bucket B are people that fall in the middle in terms of how helpful they may be to your business. They know you and your work at least on a general level and would probably give you a recommendation, but you cannot necessarily count on them to hire you or refer you over a competitor. Consider how to get them to become an A contact. Educate them about what you do and how you help people. Often, they may not know everything you do, who are your best prospects and what you offer that's different than your competitors. It is also very important to stay top of mind with these contacts in a variety of ways. You may not have the same level of personal contact with them as with Bucket A, but you can take advantage of the marketing tactics discussed below so they remember you when the time comes. In particular, look for opportunities to build your relationship by helping them in some way.

• Bucket C consists of individuals that you don't know well. Maybe they are in the same networking group or you have a friend or colleague in common, but you don't have a real relationship. You should add these people to your email database, connect on social media and share content with them as discussed below. However, if you are not interested in developing a relationship with them at this time, then you don't need to expend extra effort on the tactics discussed for Bucket A and B contacts.

Communicate why someone should hire or refer you

All businesses have competitors, and they are easy to find thanks to the internet. That's why it is important to identify your unique selling proposition (USP) and unique value proposition (UVP). Your USP is a statement about your competitive advantages – why someone should hire you over your competitors. Your UVP focuses on the benefits your audience can expect from working with you – what value you add to the relationship and how you help. You must be able to articulate these statements in a way that people will understand, remember and repeat to others to spread your brand.

Unfortunately, many business owners and professionals don't know what exactly makes them different. If asked, they rely on generic overused statements like they care about clients and are responsive to their needs. However, if you don't stand out, it is easy to be forgotten by referral sources or lose out to others that can make a strong case for choosing them over you. Be specific about your differentiators and why they matter to prospects. For example, focus on a niche. Specialize in a particular type of client or problem. Become an expert in an area. Most importantly, stop trying to be all things to all people. If you define what you do and who you help very broadly, you will dilute your marketing message and make it harder to compete because you now made everyone in your line of business a competitor.

Know your audience

When you go through your contacts, you should consider your ideal audience. Who specifically do you want to attract with your marketing and business development? What market segments are the strongest candidates for your business? Which ones seem likely to grow? Where do you have strong relationships and expertise? Once you know specifically who you want to target, write down what you know about them – their demographics, interests, pain points, etc.

Next think about how your contacts can help you reach those individuals. Maybe they have good connections, but they may also have useful information. For instance, they can help you understand what your target market cares about, explain consumer/industry trends, identify key competitors and provide other intelligence. The more you know about your audience, the better you can focus your marketing efforts. This information will help you craft a marketing message that will attract and resonate with your audience and enable you to deliver it to them where they are likely to see or hear it.

Use content to stay top of mind

Content marketing is a tactic focused on educating your audience by creating and sharing valuable information. Instead of telling your prospects about your qualifications and experience, you prove it to them by providing relevant practical content. Good content also helps you showcase your expertise, inform and engage your audience, and develop trust and loyalty. Importantly, it can get you noticed by new people as well as keep you top of mind with your existing contacts.

The trick is to provide quality content and promote it using a mix of marketing channels. Some of the best ways to create and deliver content include the following:

• **Email newsletter.** A newsletter is a low-cost and effective way to remind your contacts about your expertise and share useful information with them. Even if they don't read the whole email, your name is showing up in their inbox on a regular basis.

• **Social media.** The more you post on social media, the more your connections will see you. What's great is that you can share original content as well as relevant articles other people have written. However, don't share junk. The key is to provide information that is useful and/or interesting *to your audience.*

• **Blogging.** A blog is a wonderful way to build credibility and each post is fuel for your social media and email marketing. This content is also great for search engine optimization and driving traffic back to your website where someone can learn more about you.

• **Book/eBook.** Creating in-depth long-form content can help establish you as an expert and stand out from the competition. In addition, you can require people to give you their contact information to obtain the book, which makes it a useful tool for generating and nurturing leads.

• **Third-party articles and speaking engagements.** When you write for third party publications or get invited to speak to groups, it's another chance for contacts to be reminded of you. Importantly, it also demonstrates that other organizations recognize your expertise. All of your writing and speaking should be promoted via email, social media, and your website so people are kept aware of your activities.

• **Your own educational program (ex. workshop, webinar).** You can organize your own event, partner with one of your contacts or offer it to a company for their employees, clients, or contacts. As long as you provide good information, your own program can be as credible as one offered by an independent organization.

• **Video.** Studies show that consumers often prefer to get information from video, rather than text. In addition, video is more likely to be remembered and results in more views and engagement on social media than written content. It is also a great way to stand out since in many industries there is still little use of video.

Give first, then ask for help

There's the old adage that it's better to give than to receive. That's true in your personal life and business. Helping people in a business setting can reap substantial rewards personally and financially. It enables you to build stronger relationships with others which can make your work and personal life more fulfilling as well as eventually lead to business.

The first and most important thing is to ask your contacts how you can help them. Are they looking to meet certain types of people, spread the word about an event, find speaking opportunities, or get an internship for their child?

Next, be a connector. It's good practice when you meet or reconnect with someone to think about whether you could make a beneficial introduction. This isn't about sending them business. It's about bringing together individuals who may have similar or complementary interests.

Other ways you may be able to help include writing an online review or recommendation or sharing content written by or about your contacts (ex. article, media mention, etc.). You can also offer to provide free advice or consults if they need assistance in your area of expertise.

In all of these cases, your contacts will be appreciative of your help and likely will both remember your assistance and reciprocate in the future.

Conclusion

You should never neglect marketing to new audiences. There will always be natural attrition among your existing contacts as well as diminishing returns as you eventually exhaust your efforts. As a result, you want to have a plan for expanding your reach. However, don't forget about who you already know. Many business owners and professionals have barely scratched the surface leveraging their existing contacts. They expect that these people will just remember them when the time comes, but most of us know more than one person who does the same kind of work. Why should your contacts think of you first? You have to give them a reason and keep at it constantly.

Edie Reinhardt is Principal of RDT Content Marketing LLC, a marketing consulting firm specializing in helping professional service firms grow their business. A former practicing attorney, she understands the marketing challenges of these firms and their concerns about the image they want to present. She works with firms to showcase their expertise, differentiate their brand and successfully target their marketing so they can attract more clients. Her services include marketing strategy, content development, social media and websites.

Active in the industry, Edie is on the board of the *Public Relations Professionals of Long Island* and a member of the *Legal Marketing Association* and *Social Media Association*. She is also chair of the Women in Law committee and former co-chair of the Attorney-Accountant Committee of the *Nassau County Bar Association*. In 2017, she received the Excellence in Communications Award by *Long Island Business News*.

Edie speaks to and writes extensively for professional and business organizations, educating firms on how to make the most of their marketing resources. To learn more about her and read her blog and articles, visit https://www.rdtcontentmarketing.com/.

Connect with Edie on LinkedIn and Twitter.

How I Overcame Adversity (aka House Fire and Divorce)

Christina Shaw

I don't mean for this post to sound casual or indifferent because, clearly, both of these circumstances were life-changing. Still, with the passage of time, I've gotten an even greater perspective on what helped me to push through two of the most difficult times in my life.

Let's start with a basic understanding. I hope that no one ever has to go through what happened to me, but unfortunately, bad "stuff" happens to all of us. Some of the bad "stuff" can be nothing more than a flat tire, a missed flight, or a toddler's temper tantrum in the supermarket. Annoying, yes, but life-changing, probably not so much.

But a house fire that destroys your home and all of your possessions, or a divorce that breaks apart a life that has been created, I would hasten to say that's the real big "stuff" or at least it was for me.

So, what's the secret to coming through both situations as unscathed as possible? Well, here's what worked for me:

When my home burned down, my first and frankly, only, thought was that my family was safe. We didn't have our home, but we had each other and did not suffer any injury. At that point, everything else seemed insignificant.

I knew that I had a strong support group and I'd be able to lean on their generosity until I got back on my feet. That means my Mom put us up until we found a rental home and was ready to pitch in as much as needed to help out with the girls. My friends stepped up to the plate and offered clothes, toys, other things to tide us over until the major shopping could begin.

Because I'm an Allstate agent, I knew that I had excellent coverage, and I also knew how to start the claims process. I didn't waste a moment and found that being active was also a great help to my mental health.

The fire was no one's fault, and I didn't waste a second playing the blame game. I have always found looking around for someone to blame to be a waste of time and energy and when the circumstances require that you reach deep into your storehouse of energy, you realize you can't waste one iota of it.

But a fire is different than a divorce with divorce being much more personal and emotionally damaging than the loss of material items.

Here too I found myself leaning on family and friends for their support and love, and to hear me out when I needed to vent.

My major focus in both situations was my young children and I wanted to make certain they experienced as little upheaval as possible.

In my divorce, I made certain to stay positive and friendly when discussing my soon-to-be ex-husband. He was and is a good Dad and I never wanted to spoil the relationship my girls have with their father. It might not have worked out for us, but that didn't mean they couldn't experience the love and affection that their Dad was more than willing to give them.

I rebuilt our home that burned down, so my girls could return to the house they remembered. My ex-husband and I determined that joint custody was best for the girls, and we agreed to be as flexible as possible. The fact that we live down the street from each other may sound horrible for some, but the fact that the girls can bike down to give their Dad some home-baked cookies is a big plus that can make any discomfort easily accepted.

As for what plays out in my head. I'm a positive and optimistic person and I find no pleasure in being unhappy. Still, I have those moments too, and what moves me out of my funk are the following:

Exercise, including running, yoga, and my trusty Peloton

Meditation, to help settle my mind and enable me the opportunity to "just be"

Work, to keep me active and focused on helping others because that is what I do best

Friends, family, and my partner, because I love them, they love me and really, what more do you need

I hope you NEVER have to experience either a fire or divorce, but what I have just suggested can help in all situations. Do you have any suggestions to share?

My journey with Allstate started in 1999 while I attended college. My major was Communications, with a minor in Business, and never in my wildest imagination did I think I'd wind up buying the agency just 10 years later.

I found that I loved insurance and leveraged my love of communications and business and put them both to work on behalf of my customers.

It's been an incredible journey.

I've earned many awards at Allstate but in 2014, I had the honor of winning the prestigious Ray Lynch Award. The Award is awarded to one agent each year out of 10,000 Allstate agents and without question, it's been the highlight of my career to date.

What's most special about this award is that it recognizes some of the things that I am most passionate about, those being community service and supporting charitable institutions both financially and by volunteering.

Of course, it would be absurd to discuss Christina Shaw, the Allstate agency owner, without mentioning Christina Shaw, loving Mom to two amazing young daughters.

Mia (age 9) and Mackie (age 6) are my heart and soul and provide me with the focus, energy and drive I need when I am working with my team, clients, or organizations I support.

It is 100% true that they are the impetus that propels me each day, making me smile, giving me purpose, and fueling my passion for what I do.

Write Well, Get Noticed: 17 Tips for Writing Awesome Content
Sue Toth

Conflicting messages about content abound all over the Internet. On the one hand, we're told that humans have an attention span of about eight seconds, a second shorter than a goldfish! On the other hand, we're constantly bombarded with the message that "content is king." You have to have content, people want to know all about you ... and on it goes. What's a business owner to do?

You're going to heed both of these warnings, actually. "But how?" you may ask. You're going to use the words you need to use, but present them in such a way that your reader will see them, read them, and pay attention to them. Your readers will get what they want, which is information about you and your business, and you'll get what you want, which is increased sales for your business. Ready for a win/win? Okay, let's go.

1. Know Your Customer: Before you even put pen to paper (or fingers to keyboard), you need to make sure you know your customers. I mean, really know them. Who are they? Where do they hang out? What do they like to do? How do they spend their money? What are they looking for before they buy? What are they looking for from you? Gather all of this information before you start writing anything. Take notes. Make yourself a profile of your best customers, so that you know how to serve them, and you can target your words to their needs.

2. Plan, Plan, Plan: Now that you know your customers, you can start targeting your messages right to them. You've figured out what they need. Now figure out how and when they need it. Plan your messaging ahead by using an editorial calendar. If you Google the term "editorial calendar," you'll come up with a wealth of templates that you can use. Once you've found one you like, fill it in. Go at least six months in advance, even a year if possible. You can always add to it at the last minute if need be, but once you have a basic plan in place, you won't be scrambling at the last minute trying to think of what you're going to say in your blog this month.

3. Be Timely: When you're planning, of course you'll want to plan your promotions around holidays, special days, whatever fits your business model and your customer base. But what about those months when you don't have anything special to talk about? Do some research. Find timely topics related to your business and write about them. Check out studies about your products, funny celebration days related to your industry (National Grammar Day is a big one for me), or anything else your customers might want to know. You can fill in those blank spots on your editorial calendar with information that will be relevant to your customers and their needs.

4. Time to Write: Now that you're armed with all this pertinent information, you're ready to actually start writing. When you do, pretend that you're chatting to a friend. Be conversational. You should write the way you talk. That doesn't mean you can go off on tangents. Get to the point, but do it in a friendly manner that your customers will relate to. They want to know you, so use your special style to charm them!

5. Start with an Attention-Grabbing Headline: you want to draw your readers in with the very first words you say. Wow them at the very beginning of your piece, and you've almost guaranteed that they will continue reading. Bore them, and they may move along to something more exciting or interesting.

6. Don't be Salesy: Remember that getting customers is all about building relationships. If you write the equivalent of "buy my product" over and over again, even if you use slightly different language, you won't get too far with your customers. You know how you don't like to be pushed when you're shopping for something? Your customers don't either. You want to provide information with a call to action, not a sales pitch.

. . .

7. Provide Value: Don't forget, customers most likely have a lot of places they can go to buy what you are selling. You have to set yourself apart by offering them something just a little extra. It might be a free white paper or free shipping or some extra tips on your website about how to best use your product or service. Giving away a little bit of knowledge or something for free will help you gain your customers' trust and goodwill.

8. Don't Use Jargon: Most industries have a set of terms that are frequently used and well known by those who work in that industry. That doesn't mean your customers will know their meaning! When you're writing, make sure you use language that anyone will understand, no matter how much or little they know about your industry.

9. Don't Forget Your SEO: What's that? Jargon? Oops! SEO is search engine optimization. Using SEO words will ensure that your company will appear at or close to the top of a web search for your product. If you were searching for your product or service, what words would you use? Try to use them throughout your writing. There are online tools that can help you figure out the best keywords for your product or service. You can also hire a specialist to help you with this. Once you've figured out what those best words are, use them in your writing.

10. But Don't Overuse Keywords: If you use your keywords too often, you'll succeed in doing two things: first of all, you'll annoy the search engines and be accused of spamming.

Second, you'll really annoy your readers, who you are hoping will become your customers. That's the last thing you want to do.

11. Make Your Content Eye-Catching: Most people don't want to read paragraph after paragraph of "stuff." Break up your content with headlines, headings at the beginning of paragraphs, bullet points, lists, or photos. The easier you make your content to read, the more people will read it.

12. Keep It Short: Remember that eight-second attention span factoid from the beginning of this chapter? Keep that in mind when you are doing your writing. Blog posts should rarely, if ever, go more than 500 words. Any longer than that, and you risk losing your reader. And once they click away, chances are they won't click back. So grab their attention in the beginning with a great headline, keep their attention with lists or bullet points, and get to your point quickly. Don't keep your readers waiting for what they need to find out.

13. Write Like a Journalist: Try to answer the five Ws and H (who, what, when, where, why, and how) near the top of your content. This gives readers all the facts they need right away. Then, even if they choose to read on, they'll have the most important information. If they have all the good stuff, it's a good bet they will want to read on to find out more.

14. Write Regularly: Once you've started blogging, stick with it. Choose a schedule that feels comfortable to you and stick with it. If your readers get used to hearing from you once a month, and then you disappear for a few months, you may not get those readers back.

15. Always Include a Call to Action: While you want your content to be informational, educational, and valuable, you still want your potential customers to know where and how they can find you. So all of your content should end with a call to action. Make it catchy and related to what you've written about, but be sure it includes your email address and/or phone number.

16. Edit Your Work: Or have someone do it for you. There's nothing that harms your credibility more quickly than copy that contains mistakes. The best way to edit your work is not to do it on your own at all but let someone else do it for you. Rest assured that another set of eyes will find a mistake or two that you missed. If that's not possible, try to give yourself some time away from the piece. Even if it's only an hour, once you come back to it with a clear head, you may see something that you missed the first time. You can also try changing the font on your computer and reread the work or read it backwards. All of these things will help you find a misspelled word or missing period at the end of a sentence; they will hopefully help you avoid embarrassment once you've hit that "post" button.

17. Don't Forget to Respond to Your Readers: When readers leave a comment on a blog post or on your website, be sure to respond. Thank them for positive comments, and always respond politely. Above all else, don't respond negatively to a negative comment and start an online war of words. But don't ignore it either. If there's a negative comment on a post, reach out to the commenter offline to resolve the issue.

Now that you have these tips, get started! Write a blog post! Put it on your site! Let your customers know how great you are at what you do!

Sue Toth has had a devotion to the written word ever since she learned to read. The way messages are presented and received is her passion. Sue wants to help you be sure your message is presented in the best light, so that your potential customers will read it and act on it.

In addition to helping you get your words out effectively, Sue will make sure they are polished, professional, and error-free. Not only is your message important, but the way it is presented is crucial as well. Errors harm your credibility, and Sue will work hard to make sure that errors don't happen.

Sue's experience with words spans nearly three decades. She has worked as a reporter, feature writer, and editor. In addition to business writing, Sue is also an editor of fiction and nonfiction books, including a wide variety of genres and topics. She also teaches journalism and writing at Bergen Community College in New Jersey. Sue has worked with undergraduate and graduate students at New York University, Fairleigh Dickinson University, Montclair State University, and William Paterson University.

www.suetoth.com

https://www.facebook.com/suetothediting

https://www.linkedin.com/in/suetoth/

https://twitter.com/editorsuetoth

https://www.instagram.com/suetothediting/

www.ingramcontent.com/pod-product-compliance
Lightning Source LLC
Chambersburg PA
CBHW071707210326
41597CB00017B/2380